MW00900217

May Day:
Recovering Humor from a Stroke

May Day[1]

Recovering Humor from a Stroke

Anna Marie Porter

"If we didn't laugh we'd cry."

PorterWorks
2015

[1] Aviation distress call based on the French phrase *venez* ***m'aider***, meaning "come *help me*" or ancient pagan celebration of spring.

This is a work of non-fiction.
Some names and identifying details have been changed.

First Printing: 2015

ISBN 978-1-329-33702-2

PorterWorks
19126 Soundview Drive NW
Stanwood WA 98292

www.porterworks.com

Ordering Information:

Special discounts are available on quantity purchases by corporations, associations, educators, and others. For details, contact the publisher at the above listed address.

U.S. trade bookstores and wholesalers: Please contact PorterWorks, Tel: (360) 631-5631 or email operations@porterworks.com

Published in the United States

Dedication

For David, Sean, Laurie, Kyle, Scot & Mattie

With thanks to Jackie, Sophie and Skipper whose therapy was the best available

In loving memory of Carl, the one person who truly "got" me, was there when I needed him and knew when to leave me alone to try on my own

Twenty-four Little Hours

What a diff'rence a day made.
Twenty-four little hours
Brought the sun and the flowers
Where there used to be rain.[2]

---

[2] Song lyrics from "What A Diff'rence A Day Made," Maria Grever and Stanley Adams, 1934

Contents

Acknowledgements .... **xi**

Preface .... **xiii**

Introduction **1**

The Hospital Chronicles **13**

It's Called Therapy. Get Some! **29**

Home Again, Home Again **81**

The Search for the Cure **123**

Life as a Gimp **178**

Epilogue **219**

Acknowledgements

First, thanks to all of the friends who not only read my CarePages blog regularly but whose supportive and complimentary comments gave me something to look forward to every day and provided some needed encouragement to write this book.

Thanks to my dear friend, Meg Marcrander who wouldn't let me rest until I got this book written.

Thanks to good friends Pam Worner and MaryLou Pederson who were brave enough to really read the manuscript, offer comments and suggest edits.

Thanks to my family who couldn't read the book because they lived it but who let me read snippets to them and gently pressed me to finish it.

Preface

In case you missed the quote on the title page, this book is about finding humor in the least funny moments in life. I'm not alone in thinking this is possible. One of my favorite stories which demonstrates this assertion is a tale of the late comedian Soupy Sales. Mind you, if you don't remember Soupy, he was cracking jokes long before the likes of Seth McFarland were even twinkles in the eye. This was back in the day when indecorous wit was really just burgeoning. The story goes something like this:

Interviewer: Soupy, you seem to find humor in everything. Is there any topic that you consider off-limits?

Soupy: Well, yes, I used to stay away from the subject of death…until my father died.

Interviewer: Really? What about his death changed your mind?

Soupy: Well, my father's wish was to be cremated and to have his ashes spread over the Hudson River. So, that fateful day, my mother and I boarded a boat with his ashes in an urn. It was a typical cold, windy day in winter. I was wearing my favorite wool overcoat. In a somber moment, I said a few words in remembrance, lifted the urn, removed the lid and tossed his ashes out over the side of the boat. Just then, a strong gust of wind blew my father's ashes back toward me, causing them to land all over my coat.

Interviewer: And so, where was the final resting place of your father?

Soupy: In a dry cleaners on 52nd Street.

The fact that this in one of my faves should provide some warning about what you are about to read. If you have a tendency to get queasy, tighten your seatbelt. Consider yourself warned.

Introduction

Language Lessons

What a difference a day makes, eh? One night you're enjoying rare moments of conversation and wine with your darling daughter-in-law in front of the fire in the wee hours and the next, in the immortal *word* of famed Italian Chef, Emeril Lagasse, ***Bam!*** You're lying on a gurney[3] in the critical care unit of the local hospital. Who would have guessed?

May Day: On May 23, 2011 I had a stroke. Did you know that Merriam and his pal Webster list twelve definitions for the word "stroke?" And I'll bet your mind immediately jumped to Number 5 which is one of only two that have relatively negative connotations, the other being "the act of striking; *especially*: with a weapon or implement."[4] Funny how all the rest of the definitions for stroke seem at worst benign and at best a sign of athleticism. But you were right: I didn't have a "stroke of luck" or a "strong backhand stroke." I had the kind of stroke that most people associate with old, overweight, unhealthy individuals. Come on, admit it. We all do it. We have been conditioned to think that all strokes are caused by poor dietary habits, which lead to fat deposits, which lead to plaque, which lead to clots, which make a mad dash for the brain causing "sudden diminution or loss of consciousness, sensation, and voluntary motion …—called also *apoplexy…*"[5] If this is where your mind went, you are not alone. But in my case you would

[3] Really? It's spelled g-u-r-n-e-y? Funny the things you learn. I always imagined it was spelled g-E-u-r-n-e-y…
[4] www.Merriam-Webster.com
[5] www.Merriam-Webster.com

be quite wrong (at least about the cause; not necessarily about the "old, overweight and unhealthy" part).

The day of my stroke (that's right, I own one now) began fairly normally, with the exception of Jackie. That day was to be day number one of a summer-long engagement caring for our eight-month-old grandson while his parents (our oldest son and his wife) were employed in independent film projects in Seattle. We actually began our deployment the night before; Jackie had spent his first night in our bedroom so Sean and Laurie could get a good night's sleep (Of course, Laurie's was somewhat diminished since I kept her up 'til the wee hours, remember?) before heading out that morning.

Jackie awoke about six a.m. and G-pa had made him a bottle. We snuggled in our bed while he drank and then, blissfully unaware of the process that had now begun in my head, I got up to use the toilet. As I walked to the sink I thought, "Huh...did my foot just drag slightly? I suppose it's time to make an appointment with the doctor for an adjustment." (I had experienced minor foot-dragging before and it turned out that my spine was out of whack making one hip lower than the other, giving the effect of one longer leg.) Having self-diagnosed the situation, I headed for the laundry room down the hall, now semi-dragging my foot with me. I started a new load in the washer and began to make my way back to the bed-room but now—clearly—this was something more than a crooked spine: by now my whole right leg felt like a dead weight. I threw myself down on our bed in front of my husband and announced, "I think you'd better call 9-1-1!" The time was now about 7:00.

I mention the time because this is important to know if you're experiencing a stroke (I don't mean if you're experiencing a stroke right *now*. If that is the case, lay this book down and call for help!) Of course, I didn't know at the time that it was a stroke, although I was a bit suspicious; I'm not sure why. Instinct? Something I'd heard or read? There's plenty of literature and resources out there. The problem is I don't think most of us go out of our way to acquaint ourselves with symptoms of stroke ahead of time. Luckily, the National Stroke Association has us covered. You can find the following conveniently on their Web site with a simple Google search:

"Stroke symptoms include:

SUDDEN[6] numbness or weakness of face, arm or leg - especially on one side of the body.

SUDDEN confusion, trouble speaking or understanding.

SUDDEN trouble seeing in one or both eyes.

SUDDEN trouble walking, dizziness, loss of balance or coordination.

SUDDEN severe headache with no known cause.

Call 9-1-1 immediately if you have any of these symptoms

Note the time you experienced your first symptom.

This information is important to your healthcare provider and can affect treatment decisions."[7]

---

[6] Their use of capital letters, not mine. Someone either hasn't learned that all caps mean that one is *yelling* or else they wanted to emphasize the fact that they are talking about symptoms that are SUDDEN!

[7] http://www.stroke.org/site/PageServer?pagename=symp

May Day

I'm particularly amused (okay, I have a bizarre sense of humor.) by the last portion in boldface print. As if! Do they think that most folks, in the midst of an apoplectic event, are going to pause, turn on their computers, search for the right Web site, scroll to the symptoms page, read through the symptoms checking off those that apply and then follow the instructions at the end? By then, most likely they will be debilitated by their symptoms and most likely will have lost track of time. I was, blessedly, not alone when my stroke occurred. There were five other adults in the house; one would surely have noted the time. But what if I had been alone? Let this be a lesson to you: as soon as you SUDDENLY start feeling some kind of physical weirdness, rather than jumping to the process of analyzing the symptoms and strategizing your next move, *look at the clock and remember what time it is!* Really? Am I *really* going to do that first? Or even second?

Time, unfortunately, is of the essence when it comes to having a *cerebrovascular accident* (Yes, there are many euphemisms for the more unsavory "stroke."), at least of the sort caused by a blockage. The sooner one can get medical attention, the sooner treatment can begin and presumably the less damage will be done to the brain. So, if you *can* note and remember the time of onset presumably the medical staff will know whether you got to the hospital soon enough or whether you should just throw in the towel—you're toast!

Of course, even if you know the commonly accepted symptoms of stroke you can't always count on them being present or obvious. Nearly five years earlier I suffered, what was at the time determined to be, a transient ischemic (is-*skeem*-ick) attack (TIA). I know—three more new words to learn. And you thought this book was going to be boring.

Okay, so *what is* a TIA really? The American Stroke Association offers this menacing definition:

"*While transient ischemic attack (TIA) is often labeled "mini-stroke," it is more accurately characterized as a "warning stroke," a warning you should take very seriously.*

TIA is caused by a clot; the only difference between a stroke and TIA is that with TIA the blockage is transient (temporary). TIA symptoms occur rapidly and last a relatively short time. Most TIAs last less than five minutes; the average is about a minute. Unlike a stroke, when a TIA is over, there's no permanent injury to the brain."

It will be revealed later that this was only partially true. (I mean the part about me having a TIA caused by a blockage, not the part about what a TIA is.)

It also helps greatly, if you can manage it, to have your stroke in the presence of people who have the presence of mind to seek medical attention. I was extremely lucky that I had my brain attack (another "stroke" euphemism) with my family around. I recently finished reading "*My Year Off*" by Robert McCrum (a former editor with Faber and Faber in London who suffered a massive stroke) and have watched the TED video—*Stroke of Insight*—by Jill Bolte Taylor (a brain scientist who also suffered a massive stroke). They were both alone when their events happened and let me just say again—try to be with somebody when you have yours.

So, someone in my family called 9-1-1. I think it was my husband, or it could have been my daughter. I don't know for sure because by that point the "creeping" paralysis had moved up my leg, through my mid-section and was making its way from my shoulder down to my hand. In other words, I was too occupied with my symptoms to remember clearly. I also felt very weak (probably brought on by a bit of shock) and dizzy. I do seem to remember having to answer a couple of questions from the dispatcher forwarded by the one who called 9-1-1. Apparently my answers gave sufficient evidence to the dispatcher that a visit by the local EMT's was in order because they arrived shortly thereafter. I cannot stress enough how helpful it is to be less than two miles away from the local fire/EMS station. Those guys were fast! I also can't stress enough how important it is to call 9-1-1 if one feels that the situation could be critical. The reason for this will be revealed in a bit.

Once they arrived and quickly assessed the situation, they went into "stroke" mode, adhering to the "cerebrovascular accident play book." (They apparently *have* read the instructions on stroke symptoms and protocol.) After checking a few vitals they determined that the next thing to do was to load me into the ambulance and hightail it for the regional medical center. (These used to be called "hospitals," an ostensibly archaic term that is too limiting in its definition.)

Ah. But easier said than done! You see, I was inconveniently *upstairs* in our bedroom and the ambulance was inconveniently *downstairs* (an old-fashioned-style, "u-shaped" staircase of sixteen steps with a turn and a landing every five steps on average), around a corner, through a three-feet wide passage in the kitchen, around another corner through the front door, across a deck, and up six more steps to the street! "This," I thought, (for I *could* still think and reason) "is going to be interesting. I can't walk and there's no way a gurney is gonna go down those stairs, around those tight corners!" Luckily, at least for me, those EMT's had a handy work-around: a gurney *chair!* All they had to do was sit me up in it, strap me in, and carry me and that chair down the stairs. No problem!

It is amazing to me the random, inconsequential things that go through a person's mind at a time like that. All I could think was: "Damn! I wish I had lost that extra 30 pounds before this happened. These poor guys! If they didn't have back problems before, this little exercise will cinch it for sure. How embarrassing! They must be thinking, 'Geez, this woman is overweight!'." I wanted to say, "I'm sorry about this. I'm so sorry. Please don't hurt yourselves. I'm so sorry." Four strong men lifted me into the chair but because of the narrowness of the stairwell, only *two* could actually do the heavy lifting, one poor sucker in front (translated: toast if the whole lot of us slipped and tumbled down on top of him!) and one in back (hunched over like Quasimodo in order to stay at the level of the chair a full step or more below him.). I'm not sure how these two got to be so lucky; they must have drawn the short straws. I just know that for me the trip down those stairs—being conveyed like a corpulent wealthy person in her hand-carried sedan chair—couldn't be over fast enough!

Once we hit the main floor they transferred me to a proper bed-style gurney which all four men could lift up the last steps to the street, sharing the burden more evenly. Then it was into the back of the ambulance—which I'm sure is not the preferred technical term for these tricked-out medical centers on wheels. When I went online to find a more updated euphemism I uncovered a frightening fact: ambulance *games online*! What?! Have gamers no scruples? They can play ambulance driver *online*? You can satisfy some sick desire to race an ambulance with games such as "Ambulance Madness" or "Ambulance Rush," in which you "Tilt and lean as you drive your *ambulance* over the terrain[sic]." (Yes, they spelled "terrain" wrong.) Apparently they can entice warped gamers with challenges like, "Can you make it to the hospital?"[8] Seriously?

About now you must be thinking: how can she makes jokes at a time like this? This is a serious situation with potentially serious consequences. Yes, you're right but you will see as this tale unfolds humor is my handmaiden. It was/is often the only thing that kept me going, kept me from totally losing it. That, and also I am on some pretty good drugs.

Daughter, Mattie, joined me in the back of the ambulance with one of the cute EMT's (have I mentioned that I'm always on the lookout for suitable suitors for my daughter?) It was presumably at her insistence, as she has more experience at medical emergencies than her father (having dealt with a brain tumor—and the incumbent health issues—for years while her father, having only once been an overnight patient in a hospital, is more of a basket-case in such situations). I suspect that part of her rationale is that it gave her an opportunity to impress four attractive, strong men with her medical know-how and can-do attitude. At any rate, she prevailed (I really suspect the latter rationale worked for the EMT's as well since a month and a half later David was denied the chance to ride with me by the same crew) and as we pulled away I remember looking out the back window at my little family—husband, two of my three sons, daughter-in-law, and grandson—looking bewildered and forlorn. As usual, my thoughts were more about them and the distress *I* had caused *them*, and less about me and my mysterious medical situation.

The EMT's were kind enough to inform us that being as how they suspected that this was a stroke they had called ahead to

---

[8] *www.freeonline**games**.com/**game**/**ambulance**-rush*

the ER to alert them of our arrival and, due to the seriousness of the situation, I'd get the complete emergency treatment: lights and sirens. Can I just say, for those of you who might cringe at the idea of being the center of attention on the road: get over it! At the very least, going by ambulance—especially one with lights and siren—will ensure that you don't endure the dreaded hours' wait in the emergency room. Even if you think it's no big deal, if you're having unfamiliar, unexplained symptoms pick up the phone and press 9-1-1. The service is there for a reason.

The result is that upon my arrival at the hospital I was whisked away quickly by a whole team of people (there must have been dozens of them! Okay, *a* dozen. Okay, more than 4.) to a CT scan room. No questions asked. Well, a few questions but I can't remember them now. (I had a stroke, remember?). All I do remember is that they were running the "stroke playbook" and success in this game depends to a great extent on timing.

According to Edward C Jauch, MD, MS, FAHA, FACEP, et. al. (as in other professionals, *not* more acronyms behind his name!): "The goal for the acute management of patients with stroke is to stabilize the patient and to complete initial evaluation and assessment, including imaging and laboratory studies, within 60 minutes of patient arrival.[9] (See Table 1) Critical decisions focus on the need for intubation, blood pressure control, and determination of risk/benefit for thrombolytic interven-

[9] [Guideline] Adams HP Jr, del Zoppo G, Alberts MJ, Bhatt DL, Brass L, Furlan A, et al. Guidelines for the early management of adults with ischemic stroke: a guideline from the American Heart Association/ American Stroke Association Stroke Council, Clinical Cardiology Council, Cardiovascular Radiology and Intervention Council, and the Atherosclerotic Peripheral Vascular Disease and Quality of Care Outcomes in Research Interdisciplinary Working Groups: the American Academy of Neurology affirms the value of this guideline as an educational tool for neurologists. *Stroke*. May 2007;38(5):1655-711.

tion."[10] (Now, you ask, what do "intubation" and "thrombolytic" mean. Look them up! What do you think I am? A walking dictionary or something?)

Table 1: NINDS* and ACLS** Recommended Stroke Evaluation Time Benchmarks for Potential Thrombolysis Candidate

Time Interval	Time Target
Door to Doctor	10 minutes
Access to neurologic expertise	15 minutes
Door to CT scan completion	20 minutes
Door to CT scan interpretation	45 minutes
Door to treatment	60 minutes
Admission to stroke unit or ICU	3 hours

*National Institute of Neurologic Disorders and Stroke
**Advanced Cardiac Life Support guidelines

In other words, get the lead out! I didn't have a watch on me but I think they were pretty close to meeting those time targets.[11]

One of the first things I remember them doing was taking a look inside my head to see what was going on.[12] Normally, a stroke is caused by a blockage in which case they want to unblockage it as quickly as possible (Translated: "thrombolytic intervention[13]." Translated: "administer meds.") But on occasion—as in my case—the stroke is caused by a hemorrhage[14], in

[10] http://emedicine.medscape.com/article/1159752-overview. Phew! The title is as long as *his* title!
[11] The time target that seems to be missing here is the one about how soon *after* the stroke rehab needs to happen for maximum recovery options. More on this later.
[12] I am reminded of my mother's particular brand of humor at this point. She would have quipped, "And they found nothing!"
[13] Okay, that was a "gimme." Don't ask for any more!
[14] Only about 13% of strokes are caused by hemorrhage.

which case you wouldn't want to administer "thrombolytic intervention" because the last thing you want to do is thin the blood so it can bleed more and faster!

So my crack team lifted me from the gurney to the scanner bed, got me all situated, started the mechanism that conveys the scanner bed inside the CT scanner and..."Oh my God!! What's that?! My calf muscle is trying to escape the skin!" My right leg (now limp from stroke paralysis) went into a muscle spasm (a charley horse[15], if you will) but not like any spasm I'd ever experienced! Even though I was mostly immobile down my right side I felt as though I nearly stood up right there on that bed. It took at least four medical staff to hold me down. Later I described the level of pain to be worse than childbirth (and I've had some doozies[16] of those!). Two attendants in particular leapt into action. One began massaging my leg while another retrieved some sort of heating pad to wrap around my calf. One trick that they tried turned out to be a blessing of self-administered relief later on when the horses would reappear: they pressed my right foot upward in a flexed stance which stretched out the muscle, counterbalancing the cramp. Ah ...reprieve!

I don't remember a whole lot after that but I do remember that upon examination of the CT scan it was determined that I did

---

[15] The term "charley horse" is generally believed to be American baseball slang. One story involves Charley (Old Hoss) Radbourn (1853-1897) who was rounding third base when he developed a cramp in his leg. As he limped home, a player asked, "What's the matter, Charley Hoss?" "My leg is tied up in knots." Charley replied. From then on, when a baseball player's leg cramped, he called it a charley horse. But I digress... (http://www.medterms.com/script/main/art.asp?articlekey=34344)

[16] Doozy: also doozie, 1903 (adj.), 1916 (n.), perhaps an alteration of daisy, or from popular Italian actress Eleonora Duse (1859-1924). In either case, reinforced by Duesenberg, the expensive, classy make of automobile from the 1920s-30s. Online Etymology Dictionary....but I digress...*again!*

have—or was having—a hemorrhage, so no blood thinners for me. What they didn't know was if the bleeding had stopped. So there would be two more CT scans and two MRI's in the near future. Sometime later I was transferred to the critical care unit, awake, alert and *starving*!

Besides being focused on my stomach I was also keenly aware of all the people who would, frankly, be very upset at not being informed of my situation (and for some, that they had not been informed *first*). For all its failings, technology does sometimes redeem itself. We had wireless internet access and we had a blog service for medical crises: CarePages. I had become acquainted with this healthcare blog site when a dear friend was critically ill and the blog was a way of keeping many concerned folks in the loop on his condition. I determined that it could work for us too. Only problem was I couldn't use a computer. But I *could* use my *mind* (what was left of it!) and my *voice*. My daughter could be my scribe (I will resist—but not without a fight—the urge to editorialize!). We went to work. Nearly twelve hours after the first symptoms appeared we posted the first news.[17]

"I really do believe that anything in life, any obstacle or challenge, can be made better with humor." – Amy Poehler

---

[17] I am inserting most of my blog postings throughout the book, in their originally published form, including grammatical and spelling faux pas. (Look it up!). I have also left off most last names (and changed some names to protect either the innocent or the guilty) and blocked out addresses and phone numbers.

The Hospital Chronicles

The Overview

May 23, 2011 5:19pm

Anna is in the Critical Care Unit at Providence (Colby Campus) being monitored after discovering a bleed in her brain and the loss of mobility on the right side of her body. She is conscious/cognizant and still her smiling, caring, laughing self. She will be here for probably a couple of days.

Her daughter Mattie is acting as translator for this page. All words in quotes are direct from Anna.

Anna (quoted) "I basically have no mobility in my right arm & right leg (although I can mostly move my right hand fingers"

The ER physician ordered a CT scan which provided imagery that Anna's brain has a bleed. At this point it is not growing or spreading, and they are keeping close tabs. We are all thankful that Anna is not in a great deal of pain.

"By supporting my family" - please feel free to call Dave or Mattie for medical updates - we're at the hospital with her.

Anna is "in pretty good spirits, probably in denial. It's too soon yet, but I'm sure there will be frustrations over the lack of use of limbs. Mostly frustrated that this has deterred me from babysitting my grandson Jackie for the next month that I was really looking forward to that. I really want a cheeseburger & French fries. And probably some Chili cheese Fritos. Oh, and probably a glass of cabernet."

"Little tired, bored, hungry but otherwise OK"

May Day

People ask me if I was scared or worried or… I can only remember that I was starving! All I could think about was when they were going to let me eat! I mean, I did note that I couldn't move my right foot, leg, arm or hand. All I could move was my right forefinger, middle finger and ring finger—and those only barely. I think I knew that I had had a stroke but I didn't feel overly concerned at that moment. Maybe I was in denial. Maybe I assumed that all this paralysis would just end. Maybe the stroke had in fact affected my cognitive abilities. All I know is that, as Mattie wrote, I was "still [my] smiling, caring, laughing self." I felt, for the moment, safe and cared for. Never once did I think it was "curtains" for me[18].

CT Results & News

Posted May 23, 2011 8:55pm

The 3rd CT came back with no change. THIS IS GOOD NEWS. Anna will finally be able to eat (she's wisely chosen the pot roast and mashed potatoes with gravy in this high class establishment).

*What we've been told is that Anna will be here *at least* until Wednesday. And during this time she will meet with physical & occupational therapists - they will determine whether she will need to go to a rehab center or if her progress can be made out-patient.*

The next thing is an MRI tomorrow (Tuesday) which they are hoping will reveal the cause or source of the bleed. At least one neurologist had listed options as:
- extreme high blood pressure (which has been ruled out since Anna's

[18] Which I learned later was a highly likely scenario as "37.5 percent of hemorrhagic strokes result in death within 30 days."
http://www.theuniversityhospital.com/stroke/stats.htm

isn't that high)
-a tumor
-a post-stroke bleed
-or there could be some other trama [sic] related

Our neurologist said there was also "something" else on the scan, it is unclear if that was related to Anna's previous brain injury or if it is new. The MRI should help answer some of these questions. As we learn more, we will keep you all informed. (Personally I'm hoping this is just Anna's way of getting some attention because, let's face it, the Porter family has enough brain drama).

We thank you all for your love, prayers and support. Anna is at Providence Regional Medical Center, Colby Campus, Critical Care Unit if you wish to send a message. (You can send messages directly through Providence Everett's website, or through this page).

PS - thank goodness for free wifi, eh? :) I'll keep the updates coming as best I can. <3

Regrets? I've had a few. Like choosing the pot roast and mashed potatoes! It did sound good, and overall the food seemed an improvement over what we have come to expect from a hospital, but it just didn't do justice to my gnawing hunger or my feelings of having deserved a "disgustingly fattening meal" after what I had been through.[19] I should have ordered the pizza. I heard that they make exceptional pizza!

The Sisters of Providence have two medical center campuses in Everett; the main campus (where ER and CCU are located) and

[19]This is ironic since most strokes are caused by blockages attributed to fatty deposits in the arteries.

the "ugly step-sister" campus where they do PT, OT, RT, and other "T's" as well. The main campus has (as of this writing) a new "tower," new facilities, new beds, new computers (that may or may not be totally up-to-speed; you know how persnickety[20] new computer systems can be—about as persnickety as old ones). More importantly, to me, the new facility has menus! That's right, menus, just like in a restaurant, with choices of food (more than 2 entrées, for instance) from which you can order what you desire any time, day or night! Not like in "the old days" (or the "old hospital") when if you arrived at the hospital after "dinner hours" were over you were lucky to get a cup of juice and a packet of saltines. At the "ugly step-sister" campus (a mere 2.6 miles away from the main campus) they have hand-me-down beds, hand-me-down computers and hand-me-down food. More on that later.

I did, in fact, have that next MRI as you will read soon. But the reality is that it revealed...exactly nothing. I have always thought that no news is not, as "they" say, good news! No news is just that—no news—and it's incredibly frustrating! Just tell me, give it to me straight. I'd rather know who the enemy is, so I can plan my attack, than to be left in limbo. Not knowing is akin to torture for me and leaves everyone to inevitably do his/her own speculating and draw his/her own conclusions—which then inevitably leads him/her to respond with his/her[21] own prejudices. When doctors don't know—or can't

---

[20] Note to editor: Please do not cut this word out or try to replace it. One seldom gets to use it.

[21] Okay. By now you might be annoyed with the repeating his/hers or him/her but I put my foot down on very few issues and this is one of them that I continue to stomp on: the flagrant, universal usage of a plural pronoun such as "their" or "them" with a singular noun, such as "everyone" just because we're all trying to be politically correct but we are also lazy and so we choose poor grammar over insulting someone! Well, the aforementioned practice annoys me!

find—the answer they frequently opt for the easy out: "it's all in your head."

I have some experience with this. You see, my daughter and I are a couple of head cases. Nearly nine years earlier she was diagnosed—as a result of the search for a cause for her daily headaches—with an inoperable brain tumor, a tectal plate glioma. (Perhaps this book should come with its own medical dictionary companion book.) In the intervening years we had sought out medical advice and help from Seattle' venerable UW medical system to the Mayo Clinic in Rochester, Minnesota and it seems that the bottom line is this: a) the tumor is considered benign and not "life-threatening which is good because b) it is in a very tricky place making surgical removal nearly impossible and therefore c) the tumor is not causing the headaches. This is medical algebra at its finest. Doctors are expected to diagnose and fix and when they can't do either it must be terribly disappointing. So why wallow in disappointment when denial is more palatable?

Day 2 - "The Hospital Chronicles"

May 24, 2011 12:17pm

Dad & I arrived this morning after Anna had returned from her MRI and was being visited by the occupational therapist. Anna wanted me to begin this post by explaining her night: (quoted text direct from Anna's lips to Mattie's fingers)

"The first night, I slept as you would expect one to sleep in a hospital: which is to say, that I had trouble. Finally around 3am my night nurse Brent got me a Benadryl and I looked forward to getting a couple hours in before the MRI but my bladder had other plans, and

finally we gave up trying and they put in a catheter - as is typical I finally fell asleep only to be reawakened an hour later for my MRI."

"Ah... the MRI, medicine's answer to the symphony. Where do they come up with all these sounds, and what the heck are they doing with them. It's a good thing that the technologist (which is her official title) put in those squishy foam ear plugs. I still felt like I was in the mosh pit."

Dave: have you ever been in a mosh pit?

Anna: "I can only image it would be that loud."

"I tried to escape the noise and the claustrophobic feeling by closing my eyes and envisioning myself walking Skipper [For the uninformed, Skipper is our dog]. We would have had a lovely time, if it hadn't been for the incessant knocking."

"Back in my room, I drifted of [sic] to sleep to the sounds of CNN, woke up an hour later to excruciating pain in my right shoulder - just because I couldn't get in the right position. I longed for the opportunity to stand up out of this uncomfortable bed and just stretch every muscle - that wasn't gonna happen."

"Around 6:30 my neurosurgeon stopped by briefly to check on me and to report that his initial review of the MRI didn't reveal anything new."

"At 7am I met Dan, the occupational therapist. Dan is definitely paid to be a positive thinker. You would have thought that when I barely closed my right hand that he had seen me throw out the first pitch. But I have to remember: baby steps."

"Mattie & David arrived while Dan was here and I felt suddenly my spirits lift. I definitely am I social animal and in much better spirits when there are people around. At this point, Dan, who until then had

been kind, sympathetic, gental [sic] person lost touch with reality. & David thought I could sit up. The three of us (as Mattie had stepped out) did finally accomplish my sitting up (to great fanfare). David & Dan acted like I had taken my first step on the moon, I just sat there wondering, how long it would take for me to fall over. At least long enough for Mattie to extricate the rats who had taken up residence on the back of my head - (they all ran away this morning and left their wonderfully tangled nest behind."

"As Dan left, Jim (the neurosurgeon's physician's assistant) stopped by again to confirm what the doctor had said but to say that they were still waiting for the official radiologists report."

"Then breakfast arrived. Oh, how I long for a Starbucks triple grande soy latte. I would be much more motivated to feed myself if the food at the end of the spoon had come from 13 Coins [a local restaurant] . The orange juice was juice that was orange colored and the wheat toast tasted like: no, wait... there was no taste. But hey, what do you expect from Chez Hospital?"

"Donetta, my day nurse & Dan both confirmed that I will probably graduate to a regular room today. Apparently I'm too healthy (for the CCU). Dan & Jim think that I'm a great candidate for in-patient re-hab. I say "rehab is for quitters" - at least I'm a candidate for something. I am never good at facing reality - I try to ignore it, but sooner or later I have to face the fact that for now, my life has changed significantly. We're actually bragging to Dan that our main-floor bath is ADA compliant. Somehow I thought I'd be much older before this happened. I am trying to keep my chin up which is hard when you're slumped down in a hospital bed. I am overwhelmed and hum-bled by the outpouring of love, but I would have expected no less from all of you."

"We still don't know why this happened but they continue to investi-gate."

cling to your well wishes and will keep you posted long as Mattie is willing to do the typing."

tie:

It is so ... ie to see my mother like this, but I am so thankful that she is cognizant and compliant. It isn't easy being told what you can and cannot do, especially when you're being told to do something you think you should be able to do, and physically cannot. I, personally cannot thank you all enough for the love and support.

The word on the street is that Anna will probably be moved to a regular room and when that happens I will be sure to inform you all of the change. If/when in-patient rehab happens that will be within the Providence system. (I just hope they have animal visitation rights and a way for me to sneak in some Bordeaux).

We will continue to give updates as often as possible (and when there is news to share). Thanks again, and feel free to call Dave or myself if you have any questions.

Keeping the faith through hospital sounds.-Mattie

Okay. Perhaps I waxed a bit too poetically about the food in the hospital. Dinner was edible but breakfast left much to be desired.

Rereading these posts for the first time I am struck by something: that we began talking almost immediately about my recovery. Isn't that interesting? We had no idea what, if any, recovery might come. But we speak confidently about it. I "will keep you posted on my recovery." As if we knew.

The reality is that, according to the Stroke Center at the University Hospital in Newark[22] only about 10 percent of stroke "victims" recover "almost completely." (My italics added.) Seventy-five percent "recover" with everything from "minor im-impairments" to "require care in a nursing home or other long-term care facility." Not very good odds! Note that there isn't a category for "victims" who recover "completely." (Of course, the last 15 percent don't recover at all, if you take my meaning.) The fact of the matter is that we were taking it on pretty blind faith that I was going to recover. I guess we assumed that I had at least beaten the odds of the last 15 percent. But if I had read, at that moment, the "Recovery" page of the National Stroke Association Web site I might have felt a bit bleaker. According to the NSA, "Recovery from stroke is a lifelong process."[23] (This statement, though, seems a tad implausible. I'd already lived 53 years before I had my stroke and therefore, before I had started any recovery. Unless they mean that in anticipation your body is planning recovery in the intervening years?)

Most of the CCU stay is pretty blurry. I had tests and meals, and visits from multiple medical staff, and sleep. Then there comes a time when one graduates from CCU (Aren't the insurance companies happy when that happens?) and is moved to the next step up (or down; which is it?).

I've Moved!

May 24, 2011 8:40pm

(As dictated by Anna, typed by Mattie)

---

[22] "Stroke Statistics," University Hospital, University of Medicine and Dentistry of New Jersey. www.theuniversityhospital.com.

[23] "Recovery," The National Stroke Association. www.stroke.org.

May Day

"My new address is Providence Everett Medical Center Colby Campus. Let's see here... um, so... it's true I've graduated from the CCU (Critical Care Unit) and am now "living" in a double suite with a view.... of an Everett alley (Oh, and there are trees too). I had to say goodbye to my pigeons but won't miss the concrete and steal [sic] scenery of my last room."

"So here's the latest: I've been seen again by the staff neurologist and staff neurosurgeon and they both confirmed that the bleeding has stopped, it was just a bleeding on the brain and nobody knows what caused it. They are still running a few tests but the mood is now not about finding out what happened but what to do about the consequences. The consequences are: I have complete paralysis of my right leg and right arm (although I can wiggle my righthand [sic] fingers). If you're wondering what that feels like, sit on your arm & leg for several hours until they get all tingly and limp and that pretty much sums it up. So this is unfortunate as I am right handed and I could really use the function of both my legs. So the plan is that when "they" feel I'm ready I will "graduate" to inpatient rehab, which sounds from the way they describe it, like bootcamp [sic] for gimps.

"In the meantime I'm enjoying my spa surroundings. I have regular massage therapy of my legs by way of a "Sequential Compression System" in other words, cloth wings that wrap around my leg(s) and fill periodically with air. I also get aerobics with my physical therapist. (Side note from Mattie: who knew standing up and sitting down 5 times could break a sweat, if that's a workout, I must be a professional). "I expect to walk out of here a "lean, mean, fighting machine" Tomorrow, I hope to get a facial (i.e. a sponge bath) and a hair styling (a là Mattie & her hair brush).

Come by sometime, we'll do lunch. I hear the food at this spa rivals prison food (in fact, it may even be better than public school food). Thank you for all your love and well wishes. We'll continue to keep you posted."

Note from Mattie: It's tough to communicate/translate & describe all that is going on, but I will continue to do so. The good news is that there isn't too much news. We are all so very, very grateful for all your love, encouragement and support. Thank you, from the bottom of my heart. -Mattie

What do you do when you're faced with nothing but nagging questions? When the going gets tough, the tough turn to humor. One of my favorite sayings is, "We have to laugh because if we didn't we'd cry." As Robert McCrum wrote in his memoir about his own brain insult, "Just as grief is the half-sister to rage, so laughter is grief's twin brother."[24] But seriously, humor has a way of diminishing the heartbreak. It is a healing balm. At least for me. And it also works pretty well with family and friends, who stand over you, looking down with grim faces, wringing hands and shaking heads and muttering a worthless, "is there anything I can do for you?"

Better Red than Dead

May 25, 2011 11:59am

"Before you all panic, let me explain the origin of that charming little saying. For more than a year, my doctor has been treating me [with], among other things, Niaspan© (Rx Niacin) for a genetic condition in which my body produces cute, furry little proteins that like to grab onto cholesterol that comes through my blood. Not good if you're trying to avoid heart disease. For all its benefits, unfortunately, niacin

24 *My Year Off: Recovering Life After a Stroke*. Robert McCrum. 1998. Broadway Books. [Author's note: Just to dispel any myths, I had thought up my book's title *before* I read McCrum.]

aka Niaspan© holds the dubious distinction as being the largest cause of prickly heat. For those of you lucky enough not to have experienced prickly heat try to imagine not only your body heating up but having the extra characteristic of prickles or "pinpricks" along with it. Normally this can be avoided by taking the Niaspan© with a baby aspirin, but aspirin isn't good for people with bleeding brains. Last night a few hours after taking the Niaspan©, my face & neck "caught on fire" with prickly heat, which also caused pounding in my ears and a feeling like my jaw was swollen. This is not conducive to sleep.

"This morning my nurse discussed with me the episode (as the night nurse had left) and she wanted to know what my wishes were about continuing the medicine. She said it was up to me, but then she added this little colloquialism: "Better Red than Dead."

"The night started out well, I had two lovely visits from two favorite Cindy's & my Sophie. Then Mattie came back (after going home for dinner) and we started our slumber party. We had some of our favorite snack foods and we settled into watch a particularly gruesome episode of Law & Order SVU, then we moved on to Jon Stewart & the Daily Show.

"Then the nightmare began. A young woman moved into the bed next door and to barrow [sic] a phrase she was "an absolute horror of a human being."[25] *In all fairness, she probably earned it, she appeared to have chronic, life-threatening asthma but for the next hour we got the[sic] witness her tantrums & battling with the hospital staff over staying. Finally, mercifully they heated[sic] her wishes and moved her to a private room.*

"Unfortunately, it was right after she left that I had the Niaspan attack and suffice to say, the rest of the night was a waste. I woke up feeling folded and tired and a little dispirited but things are looking

[25] "Carol Connelly" (played by Helen Hunt), "As Good as it Gets"

up. I'm hoping to be transfered [sic] today or maybe tomorrow to my new job at the Pacific Street Inpatient Rehab.

More later."

Note from Mattie: The slumber party could have been better, but at least I got to be with Mom. I am heading into work for the first time since this happened today but I've asked my father to please keep you in the loop until I get off and can return this evening. She loves calls & visitors, so please feel free to do so as you feel led.

Apparently I'm a "good" patient. I always get told that by hospital staff (I've had some experience at this in recent years between the TIA trip in 2006, my fall in 2007—more on this in a minute—and now this.). I don't complain a lot and I try to keep my voice down. I also have pretty much the same philosophy toward nursing staff as I do toward wait staff: they're just the "messengers." They are not responsible for the "message." Besides, if you make them mad they can always "spit in your food!" In all fairness, maybe my roommate that night (like the one the night I fell and hit my head) had been in the hospital so many times—and was dealing with pain and suffering that was unimaginable—that she truly just couldn't take it anymore and rage was the only response she had left. I just don't think that helps a whole lot but everyone responds differently. Me? I'm somewhat non-assertive (which doesn't always suit me well) and more inclined to be cooperative because, hey, we're all in this together, aren't we?

May Day

Next Step Figuratively
May 25, 2011 5:32pm

Today at about 3:30 I will be moved to In Patient Rehab, I guess rehab isn't for quitters. I will be taken by luxury cab-u-lance to my new home at Pacific Ave, Everett WA where I will begin my rehab regimen. It will be a race to the finish as I want to get walking before Sophie or Jack do. I can't let two infants beat me to the punch (or step).

We have been told that bootcamp will last on average 2 weeks and perhaps 3 weeks in my case. I guess the upside is I will able to get out of these funky hospital gowns and hopefully will be allowed visitation rights with my puppy. I cant say I'm terribly excited or motivated at this moment after the night from hell. I have been feeling like crap all day.

But tomorrow is a new day and I will begin my 3+ hours (each day) of physical therapy. You will probably will now want to visit me as I have finally had a sponge bath and hair washed by my husband. It was probably [not] the romantic bathing experience he'd prefer but as they say, in sickness and in health. As always, thank you each for your continued love and support. We will get through this together.

It occurs to me now, how the old adage is so true: a stroke is bigger than one person (or was that "a marriage is bigger than two people"?). At any rate, events like this have a pebble-in-a-pond effect that ripples out from the patient in ever increasing circles that touch many people for many reasons. I was the one who had the stroke but my immediate family had the stroke victim. Their lives were permanently, irrevocably changed as well. What had to be gone through was gone through by the lot of us. In some ways, it was as tough on them as it was on me.

I am reminded of the birth of our first child. It was a thirty-two hour labor that ended up being anything but "natural" by the time we were done. In fact, we had even signed the paperwork to proceed with a cesarean section but luckily avoided that in the end. I can remember looking over at my young husband/father-to-be's flushed, tired face and thinking that as hard as this had been on me it was hard on him as well. At least I had been laying down most of the time. He had been on his feet for more than 30 hours!

This is not to say that my family had any idea how horrible my experience was but just my acknowledgment that they had their own days from hell wondering, worrying if the "glue that holds our family together" was failing before their eyes.

Vocal Notes[26]: 5/25/11

The clock is ticking; it's 11:22 at night and I can hear the clock ticking on the wall, it's so quiet. On the wall in front of me is a giant chart. Along one side are the words: "self-care," "mobility," and "health management." It strikes me that "self-care" is first because it's not usually first in my life. Not sure what it means.

Time seems to stand still anyway. At a time like this you realize that there isn't a lot in your control. And there are many, many things that just don't really matter and there's not really anything you can do about...I wonder how different my life will be. A moment in time can change everything.

---

[26] In the early days after my stroke when I couldn't write, at night, when I was finally alone—and had to really face my new reality--I recorded these few somber entries.

May Day

This is gonna be work, trying to exercise my hand by opening and closing it. It's painstakingly slow and exhausting to try to do that more than twice. I wonder about the challenge of even getting my legs to work where I can move things and I think about Jackie and Sophie and I wonder if it's painful and exhausting for them? To learn to move things and to have control?

It occurs to me as I lie here that I have achieved quite a bit in my life and received recognition for many things and now I'll get accolades for moving my toes. It all seems so ironic. Why you do all these things, why you live all this life only to have to start over again. Me and Jack and Sophie. Getting applause for walking, for rolling, for crawling.

Me and Jack and Sophie. Looking at my life from the other side of a brain bleed, it's not so different than what they are going through. We've all things we take for granted. Just being able to roll out of bed, to pick up a pen or just to type on your computer. To cook, to stand. I started writing a book, "Walking With Jack." I couldn't do that now. Every moment that the clock ticks I'm reminded of one more thing that I used to do that I cannot. And I have to let go.

But look at me, Sophie. Look at me Jack. I've rolled over to my left side! All by myself.

It's Called Therapy. Get Some!

New Digs, New Life

May 26, 2011 12:12am

So I'm now installed into my new "home" for the next few weeks and looking forward (I think?) to my workout starting at 7am. It was a tough day, I wasn't feeling very well, but I'm much improved and hoping that it will only get better from here. I have met my new doctor and tomorrow I'll meet more of the team. I have a nice view of a concrete parking garage, and thanks to Washington weather, the asphalt roof in the foreground is turning to waterfront (I'm hoping it won't flood).

I'm enjoying my private room (and the lack of a psycho roommate) - I seem to attract those... The best therapy is that tonight, my family came to visit and brought Skipper along. I'm not sure who was more glad to see the other.

You are all welcome to visit me, but you'll have a better chance of seeing me if it is after 4:30pm as I'll be in intense "training" during the day. Weekends are apparently a little more lax. You might want to call ahead and I'll see if I can pencil you into my busy schedule. (Between the tennis, massage and aerobics classes). David keeps saying that I'll recover well enough to run a marathon. That will be a miracle as I've never been able to run a marathon before this.

Thank you for the wonderful notes of love, and for your support of my family. See you at the gym.

(A note from Mattie: The continued change is good and we are blessed to have you all praying & thinking of Anna. We will continue to update you on her progress as we learn more. Love and eternal thanks, Mattie)

May Day

Vocal Notes, 5/26/11

Mercy. As in, "at everyone's." Can't stand, can't eat, can't blow my nose, can't go to the bathroom, can't roll over in bed without someone's help. Not something that I'm used to although I accept help. "Oh Mercy, mercy me. Things aren't what they used to be."

Doesn't it seem funny too, that a discipline such as medicine that uses all kinds of technical terms and professional terms like "OT" and "PT" and "hemorrhagic stroke" when they also use terms like "foot flop"?

The sign on the wall says "We're committed to your comfort." So why is it though that the hospital pillows feel like you're lying on a piece of plywood? Just asking...

You will note, as you continue reading the hospital blog entries, a persistent theme of practically begging for visitors. Everyone processes being hospitalized differently. Some people, hating the idea themselves of visiting folks in the hospital, shun visitors all together. David frequently tried to "protect" me (My privacy? My need for rest?) by asking if I wanted to limit my visitors. I, on the other hand, couldn't get enough socialization. The worst punishment I could conceive would be to be laid up in this small, dull room *alone*!

Judge: I find the defendant guilty on all charges! I sentence you to two years solitary confinement!

Defendant: No! Please! Not that! Send me to a hard labor camp! Send me to the chair! Please don't make me be alone! Anything but that!

Rockin' & a Rollin'
May 27, 2011 7:45pm

[These blogs are being dictated by me not typed by me as currently I have use of only my left appendages and typing is out of the question, so any typos you need to blame Mattie or David.]

Yesterday I began my physical and occupational therapy regiment. They don't pull any punches here, my day started at 7:00 AM with an occupational therapist (OT) and we practiced getting out of bed and onto the commode (i.e. potty chair). Then we practiced getting in and out of the wheel chair then I had to start learning how to dress myself, wash my face, brush my teach [teeth] and try to brush the rat's nest from my hair.

Then I had physical therapy (PT) working on standing and balancing. Next the recreational therapist evaluated me on activities that she could do with me that would be enjoyable and stimulate my brain. I had to say, I felt like a rather boring person when she asked me what my leisure time activities were and all I could come up with was cooking, gardening, reading and walking my dog "you don't play games or cards?" "do you ski or golf or ride a bike?" I suddenly felt like a bit of a slug. at any rate, we will learn some games to stimulate my brain functions. At some point we will even take field trips like to the grocery store where I will get to practice shopping then practice cooking something.

I can't tell you how weird it is to have to be relearning even the most rudimentary activities. Just standing or grabbing something with my hand requires all my physical strengths and mental concentration.

Next it was back to PT where I practiced swaying from one side to another and then more OT where I received kudos's for moving a napkin with my flaccid right arm. I also got to practice cruzzin' around on my new wheels. For those of you that are not familiar flaccid means worthless. These are the words that now describe me; flaccid and foot flop.

David, ever the optimist, is always looking for opportunities to point out the upside. He cheers when I wiggle my right hand fingers and is quick to point out that unlike most stroke victims I actually have some function with my fingers, this is the opposite of what usually happens and for most patients, hand function is the last function to return if at all.

By lunch time I was exhausted. In the afternoon I was visited by the staff psychologist, I did my best to convince him that I was not crazy. The rest of the day I had visits from my daughter in law, her mother and my grandson Jack; then my friends Cindy and Cyndie and baby Sophie.[27] *Later, the family came including Skipper! I was tired but glad to see all of them.*

On the wall of my room is a large framed poster along one side are listed the categories self care, mobility and health management. At the begging [beginning] of the day there were spaces empty waiting for notes to be written. I thought about the term self care and reflected on how perhaps some lack thereof is what landed me here. Yesterday, after OT had written her notes I mused that what use to be self care such as a message [massage] or pedicure or lunch with friends has been replaced with upper body dressing, lower body dressing and toileting.

Today (Friday) I got to sleep in until 8 AM with no therapies until 9:00 AM which is a good thing because I woke up feeling a little unwell and uncharacteristically cold. This should always be cause for

---

[27] Sophie, no relation by blood, is Cyndie & Brian's baby girl and my adopted granddaughter.

concern in my case as I could sweat in a blizzard. Just in case the doctor ordered some test to be sure I don't have some infection. Today was a banner day, I had a shower. Of course, it was so much work that by the time I was done and dressed I was nearly sweating again.

Then off to speech therapy (ST) just for an evaluation. I passed with flying colors in fact, my therapist said that in her 20 years of doing this work, I am the first patient that got 100% on one of the tests. This is quite an achievement for a menopausal women [woman] as the test was all about memorization.

Back to my room for rest time and a visit from Laurie and baby Jack. I continue to be struck by how similar his and my circumstances are. We both have trouble sitting, neither can stand or walk without help and we don't have the best motor skills. In the afternoon I had a grueling PT session that consisted of standing up and balancing for minutes at a time and them [then] practicing taking one step forward with my good leg and one step back. They felt so sorry for me that they canceled my afternoon OT schedule. The staff here is stellar. They are kind, compassionate, upbeat and just plain fun.

More to follow...

Vocal Notes 5/27/11

New terms to describe my body: flaccid, foot flop, hemorrhagic. Something I learned yesterday at PT is that I was thinking it was all about getting my arm and leg working but a big part of it is learning to live now with what I've got. Hard pill to swallow.

Boy, will that reality keep bumping up against me—learning to live with what I've got—like a small water craft tied up to the dock in a windstorm. When I thought—and wrote—those words, I really had no idea. I kept thinking that if I kept working at it I would get my life back.

Tucked into the frame of the glass in my antique desk is a card with these words: "Life isn't about finding yourself. Life is about creating yourself."[28] But the quote shouldn't end there. It's often about resurrecting and recreating yourself (sometimes from the scraps), over and over again for some of us. Sometimes in the re-creation you have to deal with fewer components than you had before, like rebuilding a car with only three of four wheels…

Hold the Applause Please

May 28, 2011 11:53pm

Night time is definitively my worse time. No matter how rigorous the daytime might be, I prefer the tiredness over the loneliness of the nighttime. It's really not so much that I am lonely I just can't get comfortable and when I can't sleep then I lay awake and my mind starts to churn. Last night I felt wide awake "might have had something to do with the dark chocolate I ate" so I scanned the TV options and just happened to come upon the beginning of the 1970"s classic "Bonnie & Clyde." So I settled in to watch the movie and actually stayed awake for the entire movie (which is unusual). When it finished at midnight I determined that all respectable patients should now be asleep, so I turned the TV off and closed my eyes. An hour and a half later I was still awake, so I gave in to a Benadryl.

I woke at 5:00 and then back to sleep and at 7:00 AM the nurse came in and said "do you want to get up and be ready for breakfast?" my

[28] Anonymous or unknown author.

eyelids felt like they were made of lead. I was as tired at 7:00 AM as I was awake at 1:30 AM. All I wanted to do was keep on sleeping. But the therapy schedule for the day had been posted and I knew I had to get up and be ready. And speaking of the schedule, I had been duped into thinking that they went easier on us on weekends, but they lied. I had two and a half hours in the morning and another hour and forty-five minutes in the afternoon. So I sat slumped in my wheelchair feeling weak and tired and totally unmotivated. I even considered asking the PT if I could cancel. But a little voice inside told me that if I wanted to get better I had to push through and I am glad that I did.

During PT we worked on standing, balancing and actually was able to move my right leg ever so little – miracle of miracle! But there was no resting on my laurels. Next it was on to OT where in a cruel fashion my therapist sat in a chair and watched me fumble to dress myself. At least she had the courtesy not to laugh at me. But I did it and it only took me an hour to dress and brush my teeth, but at least I did it with very little assistance. I was ready for a break. And just in time too, because I was visited by Jack the elder and Jack the younger, as well as David, Carl and Leanne and my friend Zsofia. They left just in time for my afternoon sessions which David accompanied me.

During PT I worked again on taking steps with the parallel bars. Since my right foot doesn't work so well, the therapist put my foot in a curling shoe. Yes, a curling shoe. And while I am at it, let me just say my wardrobe has been enhanced by some pretty trendy accessories. Besides the curling she [shoe], there is the gait belt, a very sturdy canvas strap that is cinches around my waist and used to hold me up so I do not fall. And then there are the ubiquitous hospital gripper socks that come in a rainbow of fashion colors, the rainbow theme is echoed is the 3 hospital bracelets I wear; the white one claims I am me, the red one alerts to my allergies and the yellow declares boldly in big black letters "Fall Risk"[29] *(I can only assume this is [as] oppose[d] to spring risk).*

In PT we worked on standing without using my hands, I didn't have the heart to tell the therapist that I am not sure that I could have done that even before the stroke. Then she had me lay down on a mat and work on having me move my right arm as with my leg, it took all the concentration and apparently every muscle in my body to convince it to budge voluntarily. She and David were giddy with my progress. She declared in her 3 years here no one had been able to do what I have done so soon after a stroke. I appreciate all the accolades but I get embarrassed when people praise me. It seems to me I was just doing my job.

After OT, it was time for therapeutic recreation. Nada, my therapist came all excited to show me how to download free books from the library onto my Nook. We followed the instructions to the letter and after 45 minutes we were unsuccessful but I will keep trying

It was the cocktail hour and my friend Cindy came to visit. I was excited to play hostess and invited her to join me for appetizers courtesy of Zsofia; French Brie, crackers and homemade strawberry rhubarb preserves. We decided to be adventurous and take our party to the dining area. As we were about to cut into the Brie, dear friends Dick and Jan came in to see me. We had a lovely time sharing updates on my progress and on Jan who is battling ovarian cancer, we felt kindred spirits.

After they left Cindy stayed with me through dinner, We laughed at me trying to remove my shoes and regaling her with stories of trying to spread butter with one hand. Cindy's sense of humor is good for my soul. I continue to be lifted up by your calls, your messages, your cards, thoughts and prayers. I am blessed beyond measure.

---

[29] Apparently, as you will see later, I should have kept the bracelet.

Frustration!

May 29, 2011 10:41pm

Just spent a grueling hour and a half trying to type my own update with no help & one hand only to have my Nook close itself for some kind of update losing all my hard work in the blink of an eye! I dont have the heart to try again tonite. I am well & I am blessed. Will try again tomorrow! Much love!

Vocal Notes, 5/30/11

So much that's new. I was going through old voice mails and found some "before." Now there's a before (that was then) and an after (this is now). Before and after. Before stroke (BS); after stroke (AS). Hard to believe that life can change that quickly. The day before, no idea, everything normal, things going as they typically do. The day after? Nothing normal. Everything changed.

A Restful Sunday

May 31, 2011 11:13pm

(While this post is written on Tuesday, via the fingers of Mattie, Anna tried her hardest to provide this update herself but her little Nook with web-access decided to fail on two attempts, so the below is the news of her Sunday 5/29 with Monday & Tuesday to follow) - Mattie

And so, without further ado - A Restful Sunday:

"I would like to start this Sunday post with some thoughts of thanksgiving. First of all, to my loving and patient husband, David. For those of you who have been wondering, David is holding up very

well. I am terribly proud of him. He has a lot on his plate, besides me, including possibly starting a new job this Wednesday. Somehow he has been managing to keep his cool. I suspect Scotch is involved. So thank you God for David.

Next, some words of thanksgiving for my darling daughter Mattie, she has been my other rock. Loving, caring, and ferociously protective. Not to mention, she's better at dictation than David (way better). Thank you God for Mattie.

Next, many thanks to Sister-in-law LeAnne and her husband Carl. They have been lifesavers for my family by being chief cooks & bottle washers (note from Mattie - not to mention: laundry, shopping & minor household repairs). They have provided a nice, safe, welcoming place for David & Mattie to come home to when they leave me here, and as a bonus, they have given neighbor John the excuse he wanted to make breakfast every morning for them (but really himself). Thank you God for Carl & LeAnne.

Next my thanks to the rest of my family: Sean, Laurie, Scot, Kyle, Diane (Laurie's Mom), father-in-law Jack and my sister Carol. It is good to be loved, and to have people to worry about you. Thank you God for family.

Then thanks to friends, especially Cindy. Cindy can make me belly laugh even in my darkest moments. Her humor is good for my soul. And to my other friend Cyndie, who loves me like I'm her mother. Her doting makes me feel very special. Thank you God for both my Cyndies... er... Cindys... er... Cindies err... both of them.

And thoughts of thanks for baby Jackie, baby Sophie & Skipper. They are the best sort of therapy. Their pudgy (or furry) faces, their smiles, laughs & sighs. And their overall cute factor (which [is] off the charts) make my heart sink[sing]. Thank you God for Jackie, Sophie & Skipper.

And then words of thanks for the amazing staff at Providence Everett, Pacific Campus - they are not only caring, attentive and professional but warm, personable. We have shared stories of families, jobs, lost loves, eating habits. They have come from far & near - a truly international staff. Although I would not wish this to be my permanent home, I will miss them greatly. And I think it's safe to say that they will miss me. (Mattie can attest to that). Thank God for the staff at Providence.

And then words of thanks to the amazing crowd of friends and extended family that is all of you who have showered me with gifts of cards and flowers, herbs and food, and other gifts and words of comfort and love and humor and challenge. I am incredibly humbled by the legions of well-wishers who have reached out with words of comfort to not only me but to David & my children. Thank you God for friends & family.

And now onto Sunday's update: Sunday was indeed a day of rest. The only therapy I had was an hour in the morning of recreational therapy. My therapist helped me fill out the paperwork for my application for DART (Dial A Ride Transportation) can I tell you how weird it was to think that I would have to rely upon someone else to drive me. On the other hand, when she (therapist) assured me that someday I would be driving again the thought terrified me. I wonder how I'll feel when that day comes.

Then she reviewed some information from the national stroke organization about the causes & treatments for stroke - nothing really new to me, however in the review of lifestyle changes post stroke when it came to the paragraph about alcohol use she said "We just cross this out. They say that afterwards you can have an occasional drink or two, but after a brain bleed and brain cell damage we don't recommend that you drink at all." I felt like saying: Are you kidding me? My life is over, you might as well leave now. Mattie's response to this was "Who are you going to believe the hospital staff or National

Stroke Association?" The last thing she did was to schedule me for swim therapy next weekend. I agreed only on the condition that no one would see me in my bathing suit.

After the therapist left David, Skipper, Laurie, Sean & Jackie came for a long visit. We had a lovely, relaxing time. It was good preparation for Monday morning.

No Rest for the Weary

Jun 1, 2011 12:05am

(The below, is an update for Monday, May 30th - written Tuesday 5/31 - typed by Mattie, but from the mouth of our lovely Anna).

That's right, while the rest of you were sleeping in on your Monday off, the slave drivers of the 2nd Floor Rehabilitation Unit had me up & working at 7:30. It started with OT (Occupational Therapy) and a much needed shower. With very little help I transfered to the shower chair, removed my clothing, showered, washed my hair - (Mattie says "That's hard to do one handed" - I said "Tell me about it!") - dried myself, redressed, transfered myself back to my chair, all while my OT Christie smirked from behind curtain. She says "My job is to work myself out of a job." I think she just has a vicious personality. Just kidding, just kidding.

Christie is a doll. She could be my daughter (age-wise) and is very interested in learning a lot about organic gardening, cooking and living green. We have great conversations, share recipes and favorite books and razz each other a lot. After OT it was off to PT (Physical Therapy). Hannah is my regular PT therapist and she is awesome too (and also young). Why aren't there any people my age doing this stuff?

Cyndie & David arrived just in time to help with the therapy. They cheered me along, googoo-ing and gaga-ing over every little slight muscle tremor. Hannah did some leg work on the mat. And then she was going to fit me with my newest, latest accessory: a leg brace. How embarrassing, turns out my muscular calves are too big for any of the standard AFO (Ankle-Foot Orthotic) - they would have to order a special one for me. But Hannah, like the rest of the rehab staff, is very good at improvising. She took an ACE bandage, and wound it from my knee down criss-crossing my foot - the idea was to help lift my toes slightly, so that my foot could slide easier in my lovely curling shoe. (See photo in gallery for the full effect - it is sure to be hitting the Paris runways this fall) [There were photos uploaded to the CarePages site].

Then, we moved the the parallel bars. Everyone had a job: Cyndie's job was to hold my right hand to keep it on the bar so it wouldn't involuntarily flop off as I walked; Hannah scooted backwards ahead of me on her stool, bracing my right knee and goading me to keep taking one more step forward; David's job was to come up behind me at the end of the runway with the wheelchair and pull me backwards to the beginning so I could go again. Nobody worked as hard as me. I had to think about every muscle, every joint, where each hand was, each foot was, everything it took to keep myself aloft - it was dang hard work. Five trips down the runway and I got to stop. Then it was back to the room to visit with Cyndie, Brian & baby Sophie. Friends Clare & Nancy joined us later. And then I had more OT work, after which, good friend Nona came to visit, and then Mattie returned from her weekend at the Gorge. I had a wonderful steady stream of visitors yesterday and that always keeps me in good spirits. After David & Mattie left I figured I'd be bach-ing it for the evening, but in walked good friends Tom & Pat. We had a grand time, telling stories & laughing for a couple of hours. I wondered if they would kick us out for being so raucous.

May Day

A Day in the Dumps

Jun 1, 2011 12:52am

And now, finally we are caught up the below post, dictated by Anna, typed by Mattie is the story of Tuesday 5/31 and it goes something like this:

"I woke up at 5 this morning feeling pretty awake so I thought I would sit up & start my day. I should never have tried to type on my Nook. Once more I struggled, once more I felt the frustration of defeat. After awhile I dozed off again and was awoken at 7:30 by the nurse saying "Good Morning, it's time for breakfast." I felt old and tired and gray. Yes it's true, even I have days in the dump.

I started at OT at 9, Christie greeted me with her typical, cheery "How are you today?" to which I replied, in a droll and dismal manner "I'm cranky." "Why are you cranky?" she pressed. I said "Hey, even I have the right to have bad days" to which she responded "No, you're always so up-beat & cheerful!" Then she once more, Christie punished me by making me dress myself completely. This time we tackled "The Bra" - it was not a pretty sight. By the time I was done dressing, I had already worked up a sweat. Toward the end of my session, a man with a black suitcase arrived, announcing he was from Cornerstone. I thought to myself "Cornerstone? This sounds like a Monument company - I'm not dead yet!" No, he had come to fit my fat calf with my new AFO (Ankle-Foot Orthotic). Yes, I have a new accessory. It is an opaque piece of plastic that runs down the back of my calf starting at the knee and curving down under the heel and across the arch of my foot. It's quite fashionable.

I had a second OT session for 15 minutes with Jill, "the shoulder expert." Jill tried a variety of methods to loosen up the moster [monster] grip that my muscles have on my shoulder. The way that Christie explained it: when you have a stroke, your muscles tend to want to all curl up in a reflexive mode (think fetal position). They have to be cod-

dled and coached into relaxing in "extension" mode. Sometimes, the muscles fight back with something called "tone" - this is not the time of tone that means you're body's in good shape, this is when the muscles turn to concrete, making it (nearly) impossible for muscles to bend or extend.

Right after OT, I had PT with Annie. We did some more practicing of standing without using support, finding my balance, and shifting my weight from side to side. This is all riveting stuff isn't it? I can tell you that it is very difficult to feel like you're putting balanced weight on both legs when you can only feel one of them. I had to take her word for it. Again, we moved to the parallel bars, but this time without my additional aides. That meant not only that I had to focus on the movement of legs/knees but also that gol-durned right hand/arm which act very similar to a limp noodle. Also, it meant that when we got the the end of the runway, there was no one with a wheelchair to rescue me and take me back to the start. There was only one alternative: I had to walk backwards. Don't think Michael Jackson moonwalk here - instead try to imagine Herman Munster walking backwards. It was an exhausting session, all part of an exhausting day.

I got a nice long break then over the lunch hour, just in time for Laurie, Diane (Laurie's mom) and Jackie to come for a visit. I'm so thankful that things worked out so that Sean & Laurie & Jack are close by to see/visit me. It would especially miserable if they were still in Brooklyn. While Laurie, Diane & Jackie were visiting Cindy, my laughing buddy came by and then Mattie came baring [bearing] gifts of more sweatpants & camisoles (and salt water taffy). I want you to know that if any of you are planning a visit, there is plenty of junkfood to keep you satiated.

After Laurie, Diane & Jackie left, Cindy & Mattie accompanied me to my afternoon OT session. I was supposed to meet at 3 with Trish, but I think Christie has a crush on me, or maybe she's possessive. She doesn't want anyone else to have me for a patient. She had an early break and stole me from a patient. Back in the "little gym," Christie & I worked on more shoulder movement, while Mattie & Cindy sat in the cheering section. Then Christie employed Mattie to lead me in playing "Reach for the Cone" - and I don't mean ice cream cone. This is a game where I try to keep my balance while standing with Christie spotting me, while Mattie held little plastic cones out for me to reach/grab. If I had any sense of pride left it will have disolved during this process.

David arrived towards the end of OT and got to see me twirl my hand doing the beauty pageant wave, yes it's true I mastered the wave but am still working on the toothy smile. Who knows maybe Providence has a "Miss Rehab" Pageant I can enter. After OT Cindy left and the drudgery began. David came armed with files of paperwork from the business that needed sorting.

*Later, the Rehab Discharge Coordinator, Bill came to make a report on the weekly interdisciplinary care team meeting, where everyone reports on how well I'm doing, what their goals are and when they plan to accomplish them. The bottom line is that their goal is to have me "mostly independent" in mobility and self-care by the time I leave. This means walking with minimal assistance. And then he announced that they believe this could be accomplished in two more weeks. (As typing this Mattie states "That's a really short period of time. How are you feeling about that?" Mom says: "I am thinking that's a lofty goal. I can't imagine it. It seems like while I'm making improvement, it's happening at glacial speed. But who am I - they're the professionals, they've been through this before. If they think we can do this, well then, we'll try to make it happen." To which Mattie replied "**** straight").*

We got a brief visit and a fresh basil plant from my friends Robin and Brenda. The plant made me think of summer. After they left, dear friend Rocky arrived with a gift from heaven: Wonderful Thai food for dinner. By the end of the day, the gray cloud had lifted and my spirits were renewed. I'm ready to see what tomorrow brings.

Thank you all and keep those cards & letters coming! :)--END--

Side note from Mattie: If you are wanting, interested, willing or waiting to find out if you can come and visit Anna, PLEASE STOP WONDERING. Come, visit, laugh, maybe cry, smile and know that from my perspective Mom's social therapy is the one doing her the most good. (She has also said on numerous occasions that she loves visitors, which I suspect, includes you). Visitors are welcome, although it is best to wait until after 4:30 pm it is not necessary if that doesn't work for you. Just know, Mom might be working up a sweat at the "gym" during your visit.

You can call her CELL PHONE now as well, feel free to leave a message if she doesn't answer. I am also working on a way for her to be able to check and easily post to either Carepages or facebook notices but for now, these updates will come as I am (or someone else who can type over 80WPM is) able to assist. On behalf of Dad, the boys & I, I want to thank you all for the support, well-wishes and inquiries into our wellbeing. It's sad to admit how dependent we have all been on Mom without realizing it. Hopefully we can begin to return the favor.

God bless, hugs and love - Mattie

The truth is…I didn't want them to. Being the mom, being the glue, the one who kept everything together had been my job for the bulk of my adult life. What was I gonna do now? What was my purpose?

May Day

Hopping(?) Mad

Jun 2, 2011 12:15am

The following is typed by Mattie but as always, through the mouth of Anna. An update for Wednesday, June 1st

I woke up this morning at 5am and as I lay there my mind started to journey. For some reason my thoughts turned to the mini lecture I was given yesterday by the nutritionist. The more I thought about it, the madder I got. The madder I got, the more awake I was. And then I just got up, and got going. I called the nurse, she helped me into my wheelchair, I put on my robe, straightened my room, pulled out my computer and prepared to blog. Of course, mind you, this process took me about 2 hours. By then, my Occupational Therapist arrived for shower time, so blogging would have to wait for later. So in absence of blogging, I decided to rant & rave with my therapist which was fine because she's on the same page as me.

The "nutritionist" came into chat with me about eating a healthier diet. She handed me two copied sheets with tips. When she handed them to me I politely accepted them, nodded and smiled as she told me all the things I needed to know. But after thinking about it for a while, I had to get mad. Here's an example, one of the tips was: eat more whole grains, foods high in fiber and legumes. I have not seen a single whole grain or legume since I arrived. I have though, gotten plenty of servings of mashed potatoes, drowned in yellow gravy. (I'm pretty sure they're packaged).

My therapist and I had a good time raging about how ludicrous it was to teach stroke & heart attack patients about better eating habits while feeding them total crap. By the end of my shower I was feeling somewhat vindicated. I went back to my room to eat my overly sweet yogurt and my bland oatmeal.

After breakfast I had recreational therapy, where I managed again to interject my thoughts and frustrations over the hospital "nutritional" program, and again I found camaraderie with my therapist. During our session she talked to me about alternative options for activities I used to do, like gardening.

Then I had a bit of a break, which is nice as the muscle spasm in my neck that I had woken up with was starting to move up & over my head. I met with the OT again, where we picked up our conversation about "nutrition" - we went to the therapeutic kitchen, I practiced balancing while standing and reaching into the kitchen cupboard and pulling food down from the shelf. With each package I took down, we each examined the ingredients and were appalled each time. Then we moved to the therapy table and she brought out an ironing board. "I don't iron," I said. She said "I don't either, we just use the board for therapy." I finally found the real use for an ironing board. With the feet on one end on the floor and the other end leaning toward me, I got to practice arm lifts. After OT I headed to PT with a new therapist - we did a little walking, but by now the headache was so intense I was starting to get nauseous and dizzy. We headed back to my room for some medication and lunch and rest. After lunch, I had more PT but we spent the time laying on the exercise table and manipulating my leg. Skipper, whom David had dropped off to visit earlier did some therapeutic sleeping. The rest of the afternoon, Skipper and I laid in bed and doctored my head. My anger had subsided and after dinner it was time for visits from family. It was a good day.

Fish Out of Water

From the start the staff at the rehab center didn't know what to do with me. They have a pretty standard playbook that is designed with the elderly in mind. I know they have the occasional younger patient (I heard of two patients while I was there who were women in their 30's who had suffered strokes) but they didn't do much to bring down the median age. Even at 54 I was a young 'un.

Add to that the fact that I have many friends and friends of friends and my room came to be known as the party room. It was literally a revolving door of visitors, the likes of which most of the staff—who had apparently spent their entire careers with geriatric patients—had never seen. The majority of the other patients had few—if any—visitors. They spent the bulk of their spare time watching reality television or napping. They did not have laptop computers or cell phones; they did not entertain guests regularly.

At meal times, most of the patients were wheeled—or self-propelled—to the "dining room." This was for most of them the only real "socializing" any of them did outside of their therapy sessions. I was asked nearly every day if I planned to take my dinner in the "dining room" and every day I demurred. This confounded the staff. Remember they had their playbook. I'm sure there is a section in there about the importance of patient socialization for maximum recovery. The other reason was that many of the stroke patients unfortunately had choking issues (one big reason why our food appeared to be "pre-chewed" and mushy) and it was easier for staff to keep watch over the flock when they were herded safely into the paddock at mealtimes.

Don't get me wrong. I certainly appreciate that their rules are based on years of experience with the average stroke patient. But I was definitely *not* average. I had a laptop computer and a Nook and a cell phone. Once I was mobile enough to get myself up and into my wheelchair I set up my field office which meant that I needed more than the one standard-issue hospital room table; I had *two*.

And then there were the flowers. Not just flowers; it was as if a complete florist's shop had been set up in my room. I don't think I ever took a final count but I know that there were at least *five* orchids alone! There were arrangements of every size and color and flower combination. There were single plants and whole planters of plants. They crowded each other on my rather large and wide window sill. They spilled over onto the floor. There were overflow flowers crammed on top of my "dresser." It was a fulltime job just to find room for them all and keep them watered. And I loved it!

So did the staff. Frequently I would have visits even from staff who didn't work my room. Apparently news about me traveled far and wide and they all came to see the "woman who had many friends." They came to see the flowers, to meet the dog, and to chat. It was as if I was some celebrity holding court. And apparently they had never seen the likes of me before. They had *never* seen so many flowers—and greeting cards (which were plastered all over my inadequate bulletin board)—and they had never had a patient who had so many visitors (sometimes three groups in a day). I was a regular side show!

They also came to talk to me. I could carry on a conversation, talk about books I was reading, discuss environmental issues, share recipes. I even had several attendants who confided deep secrets and personal tragedies. I don't mean to brag, but I think I inspired a little bit of jealousy on the part of staff members who were not assigned to my room and my treatment sessions! I earned their trust enough that they began to share little known secrets such as the fact that I could have more say about my meals and they would also commiserate with me on frustrations with the "system."

And the real reason I didn't opt to go the dining room? To be honest, it was downright *depressing*. I had the occasion to stop in there to get some of my own food from my stash in the refrigerator. Trust me, it would have done nothing for my emotional recovery. Most of the patients were not only much older but in pretty bad shape. I had compassion for them but I just couldn't sit and eat surrounded by them. I was much happier to eat alone in my room with my book. And I promised not to choke.

A Service Announcement

Jun 2, 2011 11:51pm

Due to Mom's headache, today's update will be postponed until tomorrow (hopefully). She is still in relatively good spirits, just has a mean tension headache so we (Mattie & Anna) are commiserating about head pain and taking it easy this evening.

Thank you all for the continued love, prayers, well-wishes and support.

Best, Mattie

And now, another Public Service Announcement: Anna Porter will be taking the rest of life off.

Anna Marie Porter

It's Time to Play Everyone's Favorite Game, "Ask a Gimp"!

Jun 3, 2011 11:33pm

Your favorite questions of a gimp answered!

Q: How do you feel?

A: Mostly with my hands as my one foot is out of commission. But seriously, I mostly feel fine with the exception now of head and neck pain most likely due to my regular supine position. Emotionally I'm generally positive and optimistic though I have my days but who doesn't?

Q: How did this happen?

A: Beats me! All I know is that Monday morning May 23rd started out normal and within few minutes my right foot started dragging and then the "paralysis" continued up my right side. David called 911 and the EMT's started talking stroke and I went on an ambulance ride complete with sirens and flashing red lights!

Q: What happened next?

A: At the hospital they performed a CT scan which revealed that I had not had the traditional ischemic stroke caused by a blood clot but a hemorrhagic stroke.

Q: What is a hemorrhagic stroke?

A: A hemorrhagic stroke is caused by a bursting blood vessel in the brain. The most common causes are high blood pressure and brain aneurysms. I don't have the kind of high blood pressure (and mine's being treated anyway) that they deem high enough and they found no evidence of an aneurysm. Mine was an intracerebral hemorrhage which is when the burst blood vessel bleeds into the brain. The bleed-

ing causes the brain cells to die, and that part of the brain no longer works correctly. (That's my excuse and I'm sticking with it!)

Q: What caused your stroke?

A: The doctor's response to this is not what you want to hear from your doctor, "I don't know." On June 16th for my 32nd anniversary present I get another MRI (beat that Kay Jewelers!) at which time the blood may have been reabsorbed and they might get a better look at my brain. Until then the answer is we don't know.

Q: How were you affected by the stroke?

A: the bleeding was on the left side of my brain, so if you remember your high school biology that means it impacted the right side of my body. The particular part of my brain that was impacted controls my right foot, leg, arm and trunk. My hand was only partially impacted. So this is what it's like. First sit down on the floor, bend your leg at the knee, and then re-sit down on top of them. Hold this position until your appendages are completely asleep. Now quickly stand up and try to walk. See what I mean? I can actually feel when you touch my leg or foot but it's like they are numb subcutaneously. Luckily (or David would say "not") my speech was unaffected, so was my sight and hearing. Conveniently my brain was already in menopause mode so the memory was already shot.

Q: What do you do in rehab?

A: I used to say Rehab is for quitters but I have had to change my tune. Rehab requires hard work and concentration. Most people don't think about moving their arm or leg, they just do it but I have to really focus on the task and sometimes I have no or little control. Because of something called tone, the muscles in my right foot, leg, and arm have retreated into contracted mode and must be coaxed and cajoled into extension. The normal position of my hand is in a semi clutch.

The arm stays bent at the elbow. This is not always convenient when you need to extend your arm outwards as an example today when the nurses' assistance was bracing my knee and helping me to stand to get ready to use the commode my right hand followed my body up to the standing position but was perfectly planted in her crotch. She laughed it off and said "I bet you are really popular with the male nurses." When the doctors ask me to squeeze their fingers to demonstrate my strength, I have no problem grasping them but then I can't let go which makes me appear rather needy.

My therapy focuses on OT and PT and TR and DT.

Q: What are OT, PT, TR and DT?

A: OT is Occupational Therapy which focuses mostly on upper body and things you do in daily living such as showering, dressing, brushing my teeth and hair, transferring from my wheel chair to the bed and back or the commode and back (ok…maybe these last 2 things aren't exactly things you all do daily but I do!) and ultimately things like standing at the stove and cooking.

PT is Physical Therapy and includes lower body work, standing up and sitting down, balancing while standing, walking, running, skipping…okay, so I got carried away but those are long-term goals! Today to practice balancing my OT paired me with another patient for wii Bowling! T[I] played my best game of any kind of bowling – a 127! – all left handed!! (a new career?!)

TR is Therapeutic Recreation and is focused [on] trying to get you back to doing the kinds of activities (at least the legal ones!) you were involved in before (more on this concept later). For me this includes getting around in the outside world (hence the DART and handicapped parking sticker); gardening (no, Zsofia, not alternatives to gardening but alternatives for "gimp gardening" (my term, not theirs!); exercise (walking is currently out but swimming is in!); and other things like reading, computer work, etc.

DT is Dog Therapy and involves daily visits with Skipper who mostly just does what he does at home (sleeps!) but somehow just his presence has a Zen-like effect.

Q: How are you doing with therapy?

A: Lest you think that I must be constantly on the move, at this point I can garner praise & kudos for simply slowly moving my right hand up to my forehead (we're talking painfully s-l-o-w-l-y!) or taking a "step" with my right foot (while being supported by some parallel bars, a foot brace, my curling shoe and my therapist's hand and feet!). I almost made the Vulcan sign of greeting but still can't move my shoulder or hip. They say I'll be walking when I leave here in 12 days but I would call that a major miracle! Still…miracles do happen!

Q: What can I do for you?

A: You are already doing it! Your comments here on the blog (the funny, touching, inspirational, encouraging, memory-invoking, and irreverent) – we gobble up every one greedily! Your emails, cards, phone calls, personal visits, gifts, flowers & plants – I cherish each one! And of course the thoughts & prayers – the greatest gifts of all!

Hope you enjoyed this episode. Join us again when we play "Ask a Gimp!"

I make no apologies for using the word "gimp." I have earned the right. It's not unlike the use of the "N" word; if you are of African American descent you can use it. If you're not you can't. I am now officially a gimp so I can freely use this word to describe my new physical state and feel no compunction about that.

Casual Saturday

Jun 4, 2011 10:59pm

Today was a slow day. I only had therapy from 2:15 to 3:00 with OT. The rest of the day I worked on my computer and entertained a plethora of guest[s]. This started with Paul and Brenda on their way to an M's game. Then Mikey and Bruce took a break from their motorcycle ride, neighbor Debbie dropped in for a quick visit and that's when I heard about the fifth floor patio. I had no idea I could access the outside from the hospital. I couldn't wait for David to get here. Next came Ed & Sue on their way to the Moody Blues Concert at Ste. Michelle. They brought me a wonderful bottle of wine that all the staff seemed very interested in. We did not open it. Cate and Sheldon were the next visitors fresh from swimming in their pool. It was a little tough to hear about all the sunny day activities of which we would have normally partaken. We got a nice call from Jimmy and Beth in Salt Lake and David brought a package that had arrived from Judy, it was a blast from our past; a bag of Peanut M&Ms. I had forgotten how wonderful they taste.

After David and I consumed our pitiful dinners, he and Skipper and I took a trip to the patio. It has a view out over the water and was sunny and slightly warm with a lovely breeze. It was the best therapy yet. Not much more to report tomorrow I go swimming - wish me luck.

May Day

Envy

Rereading this last entry my new reality hits home: I now live vicariously through other people. It used to be me who was traveling to foreign places and going to concerts and having company for dinner. Now I just hear about such things from others. I am getting more used to this each day. I'm not sure how I feel about my being okay with that.

The Sound of Silence

Jun 6, 2011 12:26pm

Good morning! So I'm not pointing fingers or anything but…for the last couple of days I have felt like I've been fighting off a not-so-tough "bug" but last night it found a weak spot--my throat – and I started losing my voice (which is now completely gone, much to the relief of the staff who were probably weary of my tirades about the food & the raucous laughter emanating from my room!) But I still have the use of my left forefinger for "henpecking" on the keyboard and I will use it!! And don't worry, otherwise I feel fine so the trek to recovery will continue uninterrupted!

Yesterday was a fun day full of visitors – quite literally a virtual (is that a contradiction in terms?!) revolving door of people non- stop from noon through dinner (seriously, do you people have no life that the highest and best use of a beautiful, rare sunny day is to visit a gimp in the hospital??!). The morning started with my outing to the pool. Accompanied by Mattie, friend Cyndie, and my RT Stephanie, I was wheeled outside (!) in the sunshine to my custom gimp-mobile and driven to beautiful Forest Park in Everett to dip into their excellent pool. It was another day of firsts – first wheelchair ride outside, first ride in a gimp-mobile, first skyride over a pool! (check the photos out). The pool felt great though sometimes a bit unnerving with only one good leg & one good arm (and not my best at that!) but it was great therapy!

The rest of the day was one great friend after another – some I haven't seen in years! (maybe I should do this more often…no, no…maybe not!): Mikey, Lyn, Greg, Julie, Margo, Helen, Zoe, Cindy, Jay, and of my family who was on the way to dinner to celebrate Sean's 29th (!) birthday and Sean & Laurie's 2nd anniversary. It was a full and wonderful day…thank you all! And keep those cards and letters (and those pithy blog comments) coming! They are great therapy too!

P.S. Just wanted to brag that I typed this – and most of the Q &A blog – myself!!

Limbs are from Mars, Brains are from Venus

Jun 7, 2011 5:21pm

So when you have a stroke like mine the bleeding causes death to the brain cells in the area of the bleed and brain cells do not regenerate; they stay dead (an obvious misstep in the evolutionary process!). But all is not lost; the brain can often create a workaround with a bit of a rewiring job to reconnect the disconnected circuitry. The way it has been explained to me this process, while spearheaded by the brain, is a partnership--not unlike a marriage--between the brain and the newly disconnected body parts such as muscles. In my case the process requires a renewed commitment to communication between my brain and my right appendages. But also in my case the 2 parts have been in a relationship so long that as with male/female relationships of any length--say, more than 4 months!--the one partner has really stopped listening, with any intent, to the other partner. They have reached the point in their "marriage" where she (in this example, the brain) can be talking directly and emphatically to the foot, leg & arm muscles to do something and he (in this example, the disconnected limbs) are either ignoring the brain outright (as husbands are wont to do at times!) or at best responding, "Sorry, did you say something?"

May Day

The obvious result is slow progress toward the goal of reconciliation; hence there is an also obvious need for therapy in which the partners need to be led with help to find new ways to communicate with each other their needs and aspirations. Therapy does take time, is often hard work, requires mutual agreement to commit to, and isn't necessarily a cure-all. But the results are almost always worth the effort!

I am seeing progress, inch by inch, as my brain & limbs reunite, albeit often stubbornly. I am able to push myself to a standing position, stand w/o holding on for a few seconds, dress myself almost completely alone (curse you, bras and underwear!), shower almost completely independently sitting down, take a few "Frankenstein-like" steps with something to support me, and even practiced stepping up onto and down from a "step" with assistance (go ahead and cheer; I'm becoming slightly more tolerant of being the center of attention and will work on my bow!). There might be hope for this "marriage" yet!

Reach for it Mister!

Jun 8, 2011 10:45pm

As the days go by and I gradually make progress I seem to be accumulating more and more accessories. I am again reminded of the similarities between my babies and me. Babies seem to come with a lot of stuff, like strollers and port-a-cribs and walkers and such. Turns out that gimps do too. I know [now] have in my list of accoutrement: a wheelchair, a walker, a port-a-potty and SCD (inflating leg wraps) that stave off blood clots, an AFO (ankle, foot orthesis) to stabilize my foot and ankle. A curling shoe and most recently a hand holster. I was kind of excited about the prospect of a holster. I envisioned something made of faux suede but instead it's a boring white plastic attachment for the walker that stapes my unruly right hand to it. Really. PT equipment manufacturers could show more of the sense of style.

On the plus side with my AFO walker, holster and curling shoe I was able to take steps virtually on my own from my wheelchair to another chair placed about eight feet away. My right leg moves not unlike a stiff legged German soldier but I managed to propel myself effectively.

Some progress is being made everyday even though sometimes it feels like I take two steps forward and one step back, David says that's good, you need to be able to step forward and backwards, he continues to my greatest fan. David is typing this as part of our date nite. We ate a romantic East Indian food dinner on my bedside table complete with candle and hospital linens and sparkling cranberry juice. Thanks for the love and support.

Figuring Out How the Game is Played

Jun 10, 2011 1:47am

For the last few days I have really noticed that while I seem to make progress as the day goes on I start out each day feeling tired, sore and back where I started as if I made no progress at all. I can tell you that this does not motivate me at all to work so hard! Thankfully, I have very sensitive, encouraging therapists who understand that this "backsliding" is quite common. They start out slowly with my aching muscles and then gently coax me and my uncooperative limbs into achieving great (okay, great for a gimp!) things. So I finally think I've figured out how this game is played: one day I begin at "start" and end at the third square; the next day I begin at "start" and end at the fourth square; the next day...you get the idea.

It was not a good morning. I woke up feeling I'd been hit by a train. I forced myself up for breakfast & then PT & then shower time but it took everything I had. But today I made great progress raising my arm (can now touch the top of my head!) and progress with walking (walked with my walker from the door of my room to the chair in the corner--about 12 feet--by myself and got permission to do my own transfers from my chair to my commode and back completely on my own (that's right, all alone with no one there!). I am preparing myself mentally for beginning at "start" tomorrow but now I know how the game is played.

My husband went for extra-bonus points today! He hired my long-time nail techs to drive up from Bellevue to my hospital room to give me a pedicure (and extended leg & foot massage that they badly needed) and nail fill. Do you think he may be working toward "Husband of the Year" award?!

In closing, I thought I'd share my monthly article for our church newsletter (those of you who are SALC members you are getting a rare sneak-preview as this won't come out for 2 more weeks!). Enjoy and God bless!

REFLECTIONS: Tender Mercies

"Do not withhold your tender mercies from me, O LORD; let your loving kindness and your truth continually preserve me." Psalms 40:11 NKJV

Wow...What a difference a month makes! Undoubtedly you have heard by now about the hemorrhagic stroke that hit home on May 23, just ten days after I penned last month's article. How ironic that it came after I wrote "Y Me?"; although I want you to know that that question never entered my mind nor was uttered by my lips. We did ask a lot of "why did this happen?" but more from the "what caused this" perspective, especially since I have been monitored closely by my doctor, exercise, try to eat right and take all my meds.

But this article is not about the "whys"." It is about the tender mercies that I have witnessed as a result of my situation. Merriam-Webster's defines "mercies" as – among other things – "blessings that are acts of divine favor or compassion." Sometimes, at times like these you have to look hard to find them but I believe they are always there;

you have to be open to them. Here are some examples from my own experience:

1. I was home, surrounded by my family, and two minutes from the EMT's and less than 30 minutes from one of the top stroke medical facilities in the country instead of in the middle of nowhere Oregon where I would have been that afternoon as Kyle & I were supposed to go there overnight for a film shoot the next day.

2. I had age on my side and only lost use of my right foot, leg, torso, and arm. My fingers retained some function which apparently is uncommon; the hand usually goes too and is usually the last to regain function, if at all. Just looking around at my fellow patients reminds me of how lucky I've been.

3. Talk about "silver linings." The day this happened I was supposed to begin a month-long (or longer) gig as fulltime caregiver for my darling 6-month-old grandson, Jack. His parents, Sean & Laurie, had just arrived with him 2 days before after driving out the 2800 miles from their home in Brooklyn. They were both scheduled to begin work on film projects which is why I was getting the opportunity to watch Jack. While my stroke threw a monkey wrench into everyone's plans the mercy was that they were here when it happened instead of clear across country. That meant that all of my children – and my grandson – could be with me, see my progress, and allay their worst fears. It was a blessing for all of us.

4. Not that I would recommend doing this on purpose to achieve similar results but the impact on friends has been touching as well. A friend recently widowed and struggling to find joy in previous pastimes has reentered the garden she and I share and started working there again so that my plant starts in the greenhouse would get planted instead of languishing. Another friend found camaraderie in us both having major health setbacks and was able to share her frustrations with someone who truly understood. I have seen many dear friends that I have not seen in years. And many friends have mentioned a heightened awareness of the frailty of their own bodies and a desire to make changes.

These are certainly only a portion of tender mercies that I have been given. My cup indeed overfloweth! Praise be to God!

Community Integration

Jun 12, 2011 7:47pm

I know, I know...I owe you at least 2 updates! So let's start with Friday...

Friday--accompanied by Mattie, Kyle, friend Cyndie, & my recreational therapist, Nada--I went out into the world beyond the wall for CI (Community Integration). For the non-medical staff among you, this is when you go out into the larger community and attempt to fit in. According to our friends, Merriam & Webster, "integration" is "the act or process or an event of integrating: as: incorporation as equals into society or an organization of individuals of different groups..." This makes it sound like the organization is doing the "work" of "integration but actually, in this case, the "individual" is doing the majority of the work!

We started by going by "gimp-mobile" to the Everett waterfront where they all watched me maneuver my way backwards (which is frequently, I've discovered, the preferred method for us gimps to approach the world!) up the "curb cut." Then they watched me angle around a rise in the concrete walkway and down a slight incline where I practiced "slowing my descent" so as not go careening downhill. Then they watched me struggle to propel myself along the boardwalk using only my left foot & left hand until Mattie took pity on me--or else, more likely grew impatient with having to walk along with me at a snail's pace!--and took over by pushing.

Next Nada gave them lessons on how to get me safely down from and up onto a curb on the "off chance" that while out and about we might encounter the "rare" situation of a blocked "curb cut" or total lack thereof (I mean, imagine someone blocking access for a handicapped person or a municipality not providing curb cuts for access by wheelchair!) Remember what I said earlier about CI being more about the "individual" doing the work of integration?

After a morning of hard work we treated ourselves to coffee and breakfast croissants at Meyer's coffee shop. My entourage got a lesson on how to hold a cafe door open with their glutes while pushing my wheelchair thru the entrance. Then they got to maneuver thru the obstacle course that was a narrow thoroughfare into the cafe.

It was here that I experienced my first real architectural partiality: the order counter. You--and frankly I--may not have thought of this before but order counters are designed to cater to adult people who are standing. This means they of a standard height which would make them too tall for the average 7 year old or, say, the average gimp in a wheelchair. In fact, they all but hide someone of my current height. Luckily, from a practical standpoint, I had a standing adult with me who was easily seen by the cafe staff and therefore could convey my order. This was not the problem for me. What troubled me was how I felt this new "non-person" status; unable to make eye-contact with anyone other than the counter front I couldn't engage in the interchange; I could only stare at the wall and wait. It was a very odd feeling.

After we ordered, my next new adventure was to practice a squat-pivot transfer from my wheelchair to one [of] the cushy overstuffed chairs in the café. It wasn't my most elegant transfer, as the chair seat was much lower than my wheelchair seat and I ended up plopping down into it most ungracefully, but it was the first "real" chair since…I felt like a grown-up person again.

May Day

Before we left the café, I determined that I needed to use the restroom; besides, it was perfect practice for Mattie & I for CI. She & Nada & I headed first to the women's room but were a bit dismayed to find the bulk of the floor space consumed by a large freezer which narrowed the space leading to the bathroom to about 18 inches (my current girth is approximately 30!). So we trekked around to the men's room where there was barely enough room for my wheelchair to pull alongside the toilet.

On the way out of the café Nada wanted me to practice getting myself out the door by backing against the door and pushing with all my might (which isn't much these days!) but this proved impossible given the weight of the door and the air pressure from outside so Nada completed the task for me while offhandedly pointing out that most of the time there would be some kind stranger ("I have always depended on the kindness of strangers") to help me. Small consolation, I thought.[30]

Back at the ranch I was greeted by friend, Julie Mills, who along with Cyndie & Skipper, accompanied me to PT. We practiced climbing stairs! (Keep in mind though that rather than climbing up stairs my method is more "step-up-with-the-left foot/leg-drag-the-stick-straight-right-foot-up"). But this was seen as progress! Then I had OT and more PT. It was an exhausting day!

Friday night was girls' night. Mattie brought in Mexican food, junk food, and sparkling cranberry juice. We colored with colored pencils (see the new photo) and watched a chick flick on TV ("The Rock"). It was lots of fun.

Be sure to check out the comment from dear friend & interior design consultant, Keith Miller, about ways that you help out with a smooth homecoming for me. Thanks for all your comments; they are so fun to receive & read!

---

[30] A premonition of the future? You'll have to keep reading to find out.

Anna Marie Porter

Curb Cuts and Other Casualties

I live in a bubble now, created by my little brain injury. It is the bubble of the "handicapped," a seemingly mystical world of perils and pitfalls for those of us who are "differently-abled." Those of us who live in this bubble are keenly aware of the well-intentioned "abled" world that often falls just a tad short. I must confess that before I lived in the bubble I was blissfully unaware of what those who inhabit the bubble face on a daily basis.

I speak not only of the lack of curb cuts or ramps up to the curb but of curb cuts and ramps that are located several feet down the sidewalk from the handicapped parking space. Or the handicapped parking space that is situated directly next to—and the same diminutive size as—the standard-issue parking space (which makes it useless to many of us gimps who need that "van accessible" strip of striped bit of real estate in order to exit and enter the vehicle. I speak of the total *lack* of any handicapped parking space or the lack of *enough* handicapped parking spaces (partly due to the fact that folks who are *not* handicapped but who have access to a handicapped placard are using the spaces for convenience!). I speak of places with even just a couple of steps but no handrail or *worse,* places with many steps and *no* ramp *or* elevator. And of course, in my pre-gimp state I was oblivious to the fact that if I had any handicapped friends they would have likely been unable to visit my home since you must descend stairs to get to it!

May Day

Weight (Wait) Bear

Jun 13, 2011 12:10pm

When I checked into the Providence Day Spa System 3 weeks ago (yes, three weeks today)my daughter bought me a stuffed bear that you have met in my photos as the hapless "Walnut," subdued by the fierce and dominating Skipper. But Walnut got a new name by the end of my first full week of PT when my therapist kept reminding me to put more weight on my flaccid limbs to force the muscles to "fire" more. "Remember," she said, "weight bear, weight bear." When I returned to my room and saw "Walnut" I thought how perfect it was that he was, in fact, a bear and the perfect talisman for my recovery. His name became "Weight Bear."

Then, last week after a rather frustrating day of starting at "zero" only to work hard to get only to "three" my therapist reminded me that this would take time and to be patient. When we went back to my room and she introduced "Weight Bear" to another therapist and spelled it out for her to understand I responded, "or wait, as in w-a-i-t. Therapy is sometimes about waiting, like it or not. Sometimes, Weight Bear is Wait Bear. This does not sit well with those of us who are doers and all about self-sufficiency. Waiting is much tougher than weighting. But sometimes you just don't have any choice. And thankfully waiting--at least in this case--pays off. I typed part of this with both hands.

Stuff You Can Help With to Transition Anna Home

Jun 13, 2011 2:13pm

In case you might be wondering how you might help the Porters transition Anna home, here are some suggestions from good friend, Keith Miller, which he previously posted on my CarePages. Note that items #1, 2,4 & 7 are handled.

Posted Jun 11, 2011 12:58am
by Keith Miller

Hello, people who love Anna! This is Keith Miller with Miller Interior Design. I'm coming in late in the game. My wife, Beth, and I have been out of town. If you don't know us, we're the ones who were a part of the team that put them in the house on Warm Beach. I'm happy to report that the house I helped design with them is going to be ready to receive our most excellent Anna when she's scheduled to arrive on the 17th. IF YOU'VE BEEN WONDERING WHAT MORE YOU CAN DO TO HELP THE PORTERS, following is what needs to happen before JUNE 17TH to welcome Anna home comfortably and with dignity. I've got the plan, I just need a task force to make it happen, so here goes:

HOW TO HELP THE PORTERS: HIGHEST PRIORITY TO COORDINATE IMMEDIATELY:

1. Fix the washer

2. Order & install grab bars in the main bath around the throne :) [call me about this.

3. Measure the glass of the office patio doors, order and install shades [you can probably find some affordable ready-mades at Bed Bath & Beyond, Home Depot, or the like. Please make sure they coordinate with the room. If it were anyone else in the family it wouldn't matter so much, but this is Anna - come on. So keep it as classy as possible - no taped-up blankets]

THE SLEEPING AREA:

4. See if Dave and his brother, Carl, need help clearing out the office and moving in the day bed, which should be installed in the middle of the north wall.

5. Anna will need an appropriate side table/nightstand to set next to/in front of the day bed. Shop around the house with Mattie to see what may be readily available. It should be no taller or shorter than the height of the mattress on the day bed and big enough to hold a glass of water [well, wine really, who are we kidding, this is the Porter house after all], and a book.

6. Grab a nice floor lamp from the living room and set it up with the side table/night stand at front left of the day bed.

7. Purchase 3 sets of natural/ecru color twin sheets: flat, fitted, + 2 standard pillow cases. Get a little spendy here if you can. 300count or greater Egyptian Cotton or bamboo sheets - try EcoHaus or other environmental sources with product in stock and readily available. Try Costco, too.

8. Purchase adequate bedding: a nice twin set [comforter, bedskirt, pillow shams, decorative pillows] you can find at Costco, Target or Bed Bath & Beyond. Try to find one in light chambray blues, greens, yellows and hopefully even a beach or lighthouse theme or something pretty you know Anna will feel like a queen sleeping under. Make sure she has ample pillows for comfort and appeal.

THE BATHING AREA

9. Praise God we adjusted the first floor for accessibility! However, Anna's prep area in the bathroom needs a little more storage. Have Mattie show you where the plant stand is that we can use right next to the pedestal sink to furnish with baskets or the like for storing easily accessible toiletries, make-up, etc. for Anna's daily/nightly personal prep. Work out whether it should set to the left or the right of the sink. Anna may change her mind once she's settling in, which as usual, she is perfectly entitled to do. :)

10. As a back-up, in case standing at the pedestal sink isn't going to work out, help Mattie find and install the green flippy mirror [our official term for it, quite fancy and professional, don't you think?] and a stool to set next to the cute little bird house table already in the bathroom Anna might use as a vanity.

There you have it, team. We have precious little time and I'm crashing heavy deadlines at work, so all I can do is give you this concise plan of action. I'm counting on you who are available right now to shout out ASAP which numbers you'll take responsibility for and work out with Dave, Mattie & Kyle how to get it done . We're on a tight timeline, so don't be shy, just report here, take a number and run with it. Now's the time.

Let's love these people back to good health with a comfortable place to recover, whadoya say!

You gotta love an interior design consultant! Everything is done with a bit of flair. Rereading this list I am not surprised that there were few responses to the requests. "*Measure the glass of the office patio doors, order and install shades... Please make sure they coordinate with the room.*"?? "*...300count or greater Egyptian Cotton or bamboo sheets...*"?? But of course! Mais Oui!

But when you think about it, why not? Why not dream big? I mean, if you don't ask you don't take the chance that you'll get what you ask for. On the other hand, I think many times when people say something like, "Let me know if there's anything I can do," they don't mean it any more than when they ask, in the standard greeting, "How are you?" They don't *really* want to know how you are; they are just following cultural protocol.

By the way, no one stepped up to fix the overworked washer either!

ꕥ

Life Beyond the Pink Wall & the Crucifix

Jun 14, 2011 1:11pm

Yesterday morning I woke up and the first thought I had was that I am leaving here on Friday and how did I feel about that? After all, this little room with the pink wall and crucifix has been my home for nearly three weeks; it has been my only home since my new life started. That was "before"; this is "after." What would life be like beyond the wall & scary cross? It is not that I don't miss my beautiful home at the beach but I have been surprised at how comfortable I have been here, how not desperate I have felt to get out of here, how okay I was about them pushing my discharge date forward 3 days. What does that mean? I just don't know but I am open to experiencing whatever feelings come my way as the days & weeks go by.

*I started the day with a shower--thank God for clean, warm water and shampoo!--which I am pretty much accomplishing by myself under the watchful eye of Christie, my primary OT. I wonder what it will be like to perform life's daily body rituals without an audience! I have become quite fond of Christie and will miss our daily sessions. We have shared so much more than tips on how to dress and eat with one's less dominant hand. Our topics of conversation have included thoughts on organic cooking, recipes, books, marital and family advice, opinions on the choices she has to make in planning her wedding plus the regular "flipping of ****" we dish out to each other. When she announced that she is moving to Galveston in August I felt a pang of sadness--even though after I leave here I most likely wouldn't see her again anyway. She has confided that she has never had such an open patient/healthcare professional relationship. Ours will be a painful parting.*

Next it was off to PT with Dean. I have had many caring and wonderful PT's (Sarah, Leah, Hannah, Annie) but Dean has been the most fun. He has a wonderfully wacky sense of humor, a can-do attitude, a creative approach to PT and all its necessary equipment, and an amazing knowledge of the components of the human body. Plus he's cute, athletic and SINGLE! I'm still trying to figure out how to hook him up with Mattie cuz he'd be a great catch! In PT we practiced walking at the parallel bars without my AFO and, in place of the curling shoe, some "office supplies" (Dean's phrase for his idea of a corner of a Tyvek mailing envelope contoured and taped over the end of my right shoe, making it glide along the floor easier). Seeing some success there we chanced a stroll down the hallway with me at the walker and Dean a safe distance behind. All was going well until, about 15 feet down the hall my foot didn't quite clear the floor setting off a small chain of mishaps that resulted in my leg giving way. Luckily Dean wasn't too far behind and broke my inevitable fall but not before I managed to twist & sprain my foot! Don't worry, it hasn't slowed me down too much and only hurts when I turn it just so.

After another session with Christie I was off with Cyndie, Skipper & Nada to my "Grocery Eval." We traveled by Gimp-mobile to the local Safeway where I was to prove my ability to be a gimp AND shop. We started with a brief tutorial on the operation and safety of a shopping gimp-mobile. For future reference one important safety tip: turn off the "engine" before attempting to stand lest you accidentally push the "accelerator" and are unhappily separated from your "vehicle." Then it was Cyndie and Nada's job to watch from a safe distance (Skipper's was to stay in the Gimp-mobile and protect it from intruders) to see how well I could shop from the comfort of my chair.

Thoughts from a gimp-prospective: First I had to check my own prejudicial opinions. Just as we were examining our options in mini-gimp-mobiles a man pulled in behind us and offered his up. He was terribly over-weight and a little unkempt. I found myself wondering why he was using the sit-down cart when he clearly needed exercise and questioning whether I wanted to sit on the seat he had just vacated. Ouch! I was ashamed of my response.

Soon enough I felt my own judgment. I realized that by just sitting in the mini-gimp-mobile I was drawing attention to myself. I HATE being the center of any attention. then I wondered if anyone was passing judgment about why an otherwise healthy looking, middle-aged woman was riding in a mini-gimp-mobile.

Once I directed my attention toward the task at hand, I realized once again that [this] is a Normal-mobility world. Those of us who have to approach the world from a sitting position have some significant challenges and unfortunately some of our best access is to the cheaper, less desirable items. Which means I would have to seek help with reaching my balsamic vinegar, among other things.

Back at the ranch, Dean helped Cyndie and I practice car transfers--first time I had sat in a normal vehicle in 3 weeks! Then Dean spent another half hour meticulously taping my ankle so as to keep it more stable. Busy day for this gimp!

******NEWS FLASH!******

Jun 14, 2011 1:16pm

I've moved closer to home! I'm now in a room which is closer to the elevators (and therefore home!). My OT moved me to a room with a more palatial bathroom (aka one I can actually wheel into so I can use an actual toilet!), a better view, and better cellphone service!!

NO BAD NEWS!!

Jun 14, 2011 1:43pm

Sorry about the urgent status of the last update! I was just trying to get people's attention about my moving!

Anna Marie Porter

One has to be very careful when one uses words like "urgent" around folks who are on heightened alert. I'm carried back again to the time when we were expecting our first child. We had never been through anything like this before and I had not yet seen how my husband responds emotionally to stressful situations (I can tell you, it's *not* good! While I'm more pragmatic—perhaps bordering on delusional at times—he immediately anticipates the worst possible scenario and recognizes how ill-prepared he is to cope with it.)

Anyway, this was back in the day *before* cell phones and texting (yes, children, there was a time when we didn't have such mundane technology!) but David did have a pager. I was in the last trimester of my pregnancy and I needed to ask him something (I don't remember what but it wasn't urgent; I just wanted him to call me back when he was finished with the meeting that I knew he was attending). Recognizing that any "pages" from me at this stage of the game would send my hyper-alert husband into a state of panic, I made sure he knew that it wasn't an emergency—or even related to the pregnancy—so I finished the brief message I left on his pager service ("Please call me.") with the words, "No Hurry.")

My office desk phone rang almost immediately after. "What's wrong?!" my terrified husband queried nervously. "Nothing's wrong," said I, "I said it wasn't urgent and not to hurry!"
"Oh," he sighed in relief, "all I heard was '*hurry*!'"

May Day

Moving Ever Closer

Jun 15, 2011 10:07am

Yesterday I moved closer to the elevator but I also moved closer to leaving in other ways. It started with more work at the stairs. I am getting better each time with dragging my stubborn right foot and hand along. Then a big test: cooking! I had to prepare the food I had purchased the day before for my OT: my much-acclaimed kale salad. I wondered how cutting would work with my right hand. No worries there; I'd be surprised if one could cut ANYTHING with the knives in that kitchen! I managed though, and also cooked the dressing and tossed the ingredients without spilling or burning myself. And just in time good friend Dave arrived with some of his most awesome bread to complete the meal! I think I passed the cooking test! I also honed my wedding coordinator skills by helping Christie choose her reception menu and wines!

Later, it was more PT to keep working those ever-important walking and stair-stepping skills. And that was it for me. That damnable Baclofen wipes me out--ended up falling asleep the first time at about 8:30, though I had been drifting since 4:30! Unfortunately, it is a necessary evil because it makes my muscles cooperate better.

Late in the afternoon the discharge planner came in to confirm that everyone agrees that Friday is the day! There is lots to do--not just for me but for family training--before then.

Moving ever closer...

P.S. Typed MOST of this using BOTH hands!

What I Will Miss

Jun 16, 2011 1:28am

Christie, my primary OT, who has become a dear friend, with whom I have shared much. I will miss her the most.

All the communication and visits with so many wonderful friends, especially those that I have not seen or heard from in a long time!

The rest of the staff at Providence Pacific campus; they have all been wonderfully caring and supportive.

Waking each morning to a virtual flower shop!

What I Will Miss (NOT)!

The food!

The bed!

The rattling, beeping, squeaking, screeching, etc., of the various hospital equipment!

The concrete parking garage & hot-mopped roof outside my window!

The flat pillows!

SCD's, gait belts, "boots," straps, pads, and other devices.

The food!

Passages

Truth be told, I was, well I wouldn't say *terrified* of going home; let's just say I wasn't as excited as one might expect. This surprised and confounded me. Why on earth would anyone *not* be eager and ready to get back to familiar surroundings—especially with a view like ours?

Perhaps it was because I was going home to a familiar place but in a stranger's body. I knew how to live in the hospital. I knew what to expect and what my limitations were. Life at home was predictable.

I could get around. I could do most of the things I needed to do for myself. I had my little room where everything had its place and was in its place. I had my routine. I could manage—even master—this small world where I knew how to function. And in here I was an *overachiever*! I was successful. Compared to the rest of the patients I was highly functioning. And I didn't have to explain myself. Everyone knew why I was there and what could be expected of me. And no one watched me, wondering or judging.

But out *there*? That was another matter entirely. Out there people did things that I could only dream—or reminisce—about. Out there I was an anomaly, a circus side-show character. Out there I would have it rubbed in my face every day that I now had limitations and shortcomings, that there were oh so many things that I *could not* do. And there would be many more disappointments. I would be a fish out of water and I was afraid I'd asphyxiate.

I had another revelation later: my home has now become my "room." Against the urgings of well-meaning friends and family to get out (translated: "get back to normal") I find that I am perfectly happy to stay in my comfortable, knowable home. If I ever forget why I feel this way, I am reminded when I *do* leave the house. Here things are fairly predictable: the floors are even, there are railings for all the steps, and I can get along mostly on my own. Out *there* nothing is predictable. And challenges abound. In fact, just *getting* there can be a challenge. I used to be quite conscious of wearing the "right" thing, including matching shoes. My options now include which yoga pants to wear and which socks to put into the one pair of shoes I can put my AFO into. Getting around *out there* is clumsy at best: floors and sidewalks are uneven, steps and curbs are rail-less. Even getting around on carpeted floors (Ours are all hard surface, just like the hospital; it's easier to swing this uncooperative foot through.) or around people and obstacles is not an easy proposition. In social settings where most people are standing talking while balancing their glass of wine and even an hors d' oeuvres plate I tend to plant myself somewhere where my cane and I are out of the way and I'm less likely to get toppled over.

The idea of staying at home is not depressing to me. I do not feel like I am missing out. It is *out there* that the stark reality of my fate revealed against the backdrop of *normal* makes me truly aware that I am missing out.

To Do Everyday

Jun 16, 2011 10:49am

Okay...I have a tendency to get going in the morning by just jumping in and doing what immediately floats to the top. The result of this is that I also have a tendency to forget things that I ought to do daily--usually in regards to work. There are many part of my job at PorterWorks--too many, me thinks!--and if I don't stop and make a list I tend to forget them. Hence, recently, I created a little digital "post-it" note that hangs out on the desktop of my computer which reads like this:

May Day

EVERY DAY!

Check email

Check gmail

Twitter

Facebook

Blogs

Check ops email and calendar

I've been doing pretty good at all of these lately (save #6 which I thankfully don't have to do now that we have hired the fabulous Kelly as our new Ops Mgr!) because, well, other than PT & OT I have plenty of time on my hands! The other day when I started up my computer I could see a need for another sort of "to do" list, one that reflects this new life of mine.

Now lest you think that I, having experienced a life-altering event, am suddenly profoundly transformed (as in some Dickens novel) and am now going to expound on how flowers smell more sweet and birds sing more beautifully and I will be thankful each minute for each breath...you've got the wrong girl! First of all, maybe I live in denial… but I never once thought that my life was in grave danger. I didn't think I was going to die. I might have pondered at times that that might be as good as it gets but I never thought it was the end. Maybe one needs to experience that to make real extreme life--translated "personality"--changes. I like to think that I was already good at appreciating my life. I already take "time to smell the flowers," I already appreciate the little joys of life like a well-cooked meal, a great sunset, a baby's giggle. I didn't need this event to remind me to notice those or to remember that I am profoundly loved by many,

many people and how blessed I am by that. But there are still things that I'd like to remind myself to do each day.

EVERY DAY!

1. Pray. (It may seem odd to some of you who know me well that I should have to remind myself to do this but even in the best of years I was prone to forgetting and now in menopause I have had a tenuous relationship with God at best. So I resolve--again--to pray regularly.)

2. Breathe. (I know. Should be involuntary but I'm talking about the kind of deep, healing, forcing-you-to-pause kind of breathing.)

3. Slow down. (Out of necessity I have had to do this. It has not come naturally and I will have to remind myself to do it regularly.)

4. Do something important to me personally every day. (You know me. I exist for others so doing something for just me is pretty tough but I know tis necessary for my well-being.)

5. Write. (It might seem odd to include this in the list, given my recent activity but even though it is good therapy for me I don't give myself the time regularly.)

6. Find something to be thankful for each day. (No matter how small. As blessed as I am, this shouldn't be difficult at all.)

This is my list for now. Lists are always subject to change.

One More Sleep

Jun 17, 2011 12:11am

To paraphrase Kermit the Frog in "A Muppet Christmas Carol," "There's only one more sleep til homecoming!" I think I am ready. I still have miles to go but am amazed at far I have come in such a very short time. It has been good to be here; the therapy was necessary and fruitful. I leave with renewed confidence that I will return to normal (as normal as one could say that I was!). I feel a strange "blueness" over leaving; we joked with my OT that it was, we imagined, similar to how hostages feel about leaving their longtime kidnapper/captors! They're not sure why but they will miss them.

It is enough. Next chapter; next book. I promise to keep writing about my recovery since a significant number of you apparently have no life!

much humble thanks.

Home Again, Home Again

Homecoming

Jun 18, 2011 6:05pm

Here I am at home finally! I was sprung yesterday at noon; got all my discharge instructions, prescriptions, assignments etc. and then we loaded up and left. On the way home, David treated me to Red Robin--okay, not the healthiest food but it was at least tastier than hospital food! More fun experiencing CI (Community Integration): unloading in a non-handicapped zone cuz they were full; wheeling through a crowded restaurant; sitting in my special chair at the table.

Once home I was greeted by family and pets and balloons! It was strange to be home; felt other-worldly. I realized something that I had not thought of: I'm kinda OCD (obsessive compulsive disorder) about clutter and stuff and didn't anticipate how uncomfortable it would be to be back on my own turf and unable to really do much. I immediately wanted to jump in and clean up but was limited in what I could do. Cyndie came to my rescue (she's OCD worse than me so understands my frustration) by reshuffling the clutter at my direction. I felt better! But as she reminded me, I need to work on "letting go" and just not wigging out about stuff I can't do. In my own little room at the hospital I could do a lot of the cleaning and organizing in my small space, but at home it's just too big for me to handle!

Last night I had a coming home party with many of the local beach crowd in attendance. Brian made a delicious chicken alfredo, Mel brought his famous chopped salad, Johnny & Carl rustled up shrimp skewers and Copper River salmon (thanks, Larry & Faye for springing for that delicacy!). It was too bad we didn't have enough food! :)

I slept in my little bed in my special gimp room (thank you Cindy & Dave for the bed, Nona for the darling nautical-print comforter set, and my family for pulling the rest of the room together!) with my faithful dog and cat who have missed sleeping with me for 3-1/2 weeks! Then it was up for a shower and out to brave the cold Junuary weather at the Soapbox Derby races in Stanwood (Cyndie & Brian's son, Sam was driving our Warm Beach Community car!). It was more CI fun...going up and down sidewalks and even some offroading...good exercise for my "caregivers!"

It is good to be home!

Home, (bitter)Sweet, Home

Jun 21, 2011 12:06am

It is good to be home, good to be back among my family, friends and pets and good food! But I never thought about the effect of being home and being an observer. In the hospital it was easy to keep thoughts of greenhouse plants dying, weeds growing, clutter piling up, and a beach beckoning at bay. Out of sight made it easier to keep out of mind. Denial...it's not just a river in Egypt any more. At home all of those things are staring you in the face, taunting you with the stark reality of your physical limitations. And it is so much harder to abide by the "let it go" platitude. Here I am constantly confronted with what I can't do and it is hard to keep my chin up.

I want so badly to go out and pull those weeds that are popping up all over. I want to go down to the greenhouse and replant the seeds that had grown to seedlings before I left and in my absence died from lack of water. I want to go around the house and put away all the little piles of things that have been growing without me to de-clutter. I want to walk down to the neighbors for a glass of wine (which, for some reason, does not taste good to me now!) I want to walk the beach with my dog. I know that all of these things will return in time but that doesn't make it any easier right now. I was unprepared for these feelings of frustrating limitation. It is okay. I will move beyond this too.

I also was unprepared for FT. No, not "Food Therapy" as in the hospital that made me desperate to get better! Now, FT stands for "Family Therapy." This sounds like it would be a good thing, and, indeed it is lovely that my family wants to help! But they hover! In the hospital I had actually distinguished myself as "Little Miss Independent." I was officially "independent" at "transfers" from bed to wheel chair to commode and ultimately toilet. I was "independent" in my dressing. I was relishing the freedom from having to ask someone to handle my most simple requests like opening the blinds or turning on or off my fan or getting my own hot water for tea. I have mentioned before that I hate being the center of attention (really! I do!) and I hate asking people to do things for me. Now at home, "Little Miss Independent" is suddenly under rabid scrutiny! I can't sneeze without someone asking me if I'm okay. They help me with dressing, going to the bathroom--all the things I was doing for myself, albeit slowly and clumsily. And I understand their concern but it makes me feel like I've taken a giant leap backward in my recovery. I actually was able to convince my brother-in-law that I wanted to--and could--get my own breakfast. And he spent the rest of the day reminding everyone else that I did so! I don't want to hurt anyone's feelings but I want to do what I can for myself, to salvage what self-esteem I have left!

This too shall pass. I will keep getting better. I do my exercises every day. I am back to doing some of my work for our business (having my right hand back, no matter how weak, has been a huge blessing!) and I keep working on improving my stiff-legged gait. Soon I will begin in-home physical therapy so I won't feel like I've come to a standstill in my progress.

But today, I'm feeling just a little sorry for myself. And I think that's okay.

May Day

"I know that all of these things will return in time..." How could I have known? Why was I so confident? Probably because at this point in my recovery I had been gradually *recovering* my old abilities. So I made an assumption—many of them actually.

Sunshine!

Jun 21, 2011 11:49am

Your comments and emails bring sunshine every day! I can't wait til I open my CarePages to read what you have sent me. You all inspire, amaze and encourage me. Thank you so much!

Friends' notes were—and are—my sunshine, mostly because they bolstered my self-esteem which had suffered as much as my body had.

A Biology Lesson

Jun 22, 2011 1:07pm

Last Thursday I had a follow-up MRI. The purpose was to ascertain whether there was any evidence of what might have caused the stroke. Unfortunately they couldn't "see" anything because the blood that had pooled as a result of the brain bleed had not yet been reabsorbed into my system and could still be blocking "who-knows-what." This leaves us to nothing but speculation with the help of some of my doc-

tors and the internet. (what would we do without the world wide web?!) [31]

So, for your edification, here are a few more acronyms. Just to recap, in 2006 I suffered what the hospital decided was a TIA (transient ischemic attack). It started with some classic stroke symptoms (loss of vision in one eye, as though a curtain has fallen; weakness in arms & legs). Ischemic is basically a blockage of an artery. Ischemic strokes account for as much as 90% of all strokes. A TIA is a mini-stroke, transient in nature, usually the effects of which last 24 hours or less. Mine, however, lasted longer but seeing no evidence of a real stroke and because I had no residual effects, they decided it must be a TIA (in other words, as is often the case, diagnosis was determined by the process of elimination). It was not for lack of trying. They dutifully performed every diagnostic test they could think of but to no avail.

So they sent me away with my TIA diagnosis, advice to start taking an aspirin a day, and a referral to a neurologist to look at some funny spots on my brain MRI that were unrelated. My neurologist determined the "funny spots" were no big deal but she asked if I had had a PFO study. Not only did I not know if I had had that study done but what the heck was a PFO?!

A PFO is a patent (PAY-tent) foramen (for-AY-men) ovale (o-VAL-ee). Yeah, drop that one at your next cocktail party and show them how smart you are! But what IS a patent foremen ovale you ask? Okay, you asked for it!

Here I quote my cardiac surgeon at the UWMC: "The heart has two sides, right and left, separated by walls called septa that prevent deoxygenated blood on the right side from mixing with oxygenated blood on the left. When a septum has a hole, blood from the right side leaks

---

[31] ...of *intrigue!* By the way, I found out recently that it is *the* World Wide Web; in other words, it gets capitalized. In more ways than one.

into the left side, or vice versa. As a result, the heart cannot pump blood as efficiently as it normally would.

The atrial septum separates the top chambers of the heart, the right and left atria. The foramen ovale (fore-AY-men oh-VAL-ee) is a naturally occurring hole in the fetal atrial septum. Because a fetus does not use its lungs – it gets oxygen from its mother – this naturally occurring hole allows a fetus to circulate its blood while bypassing its lungs.

The foramen ovale usually closes within a few years of birth. In about 10 to 20 percent of people it remains leaky, allowing tiny amounts of deoxygenated and oxygenated blood to mix. More than 99 percent of people with a patent (PAY-tent, meaning "open") foramen ovale (PFO) do not show symptoms and do not need treatment. However, in some patients, the PFO allows blood clots and other debris to pass from the venous (deoxygenated) system to the arterial (oxygenated) system. Normally these clots and debris are filtered by the lungs. Once a clot or particle enters the arterial system, it can cause a stroke or cut off circulation to a limb or vital organ." Phew!

So, I was given the test and I passed with flying colors! I apparently have a "significant" PFO! Around about that time the medical community was hotly debating whether a PFO could significantly increase a person's chance of having a stroke and, if so, whether something should be done to close it. After consulting with my cardiologist, I decided to take my chances and not do surgery.

This might have been a mistake.

Fast forward to a month ago. This time, instead of a mini-ischemic stroke I had a full-on hemorrhagic one. Remember the difference? An ischemic stroke is caused by a blockage; a hemorrhagic one is caused by a burst blood vessel. That bursting is usually caused by hypertension (which they dismissed in my case) but can be caused also by an aneurysm, a tumor or a clot. Hmmm...When I mentioned my PFO to the neurosurgeon at Providence he got suspicious. Although we cannot yet see any cause for the bleeding the presence of a PFO does seem suspicious. The other suspicious evidence is that when they looked at the first 3 CT scans and 2 MRI's they saw evidence that I had had some other strokes of which I was apparently unaware!

So, I will be following up with the cardiologist. Stay tuned...

I Bent My Knee Yesterday

Jun 25, 2011 2:20pm

It's the little things. Last night I was pleasantly surprised by a visit from dear friends! It was so lovely to see them all, eat some great pizza and even sip a little bit of wine! Of course, there were all the "oohs and ahhs" from everyone about the progress that I have made since I have seen many of them. They were all very supportive and anxious to hear if there was anything new to report.

Hmmm...anything new...anything new...Oh yeah! I bent my knee! Why is this a big deal? Because, in case you never noticed it, when you walk take a look at what your feet and legs do to make that happen. You probably never noticed before. Take a few minutes to fully appreciate all the muscles, tendons, joints and bones that are required to move you forward down the street. You might notice that your knees are some of the things that bend to make walking happen. I never paid any mind to this before but having to learn to walk again makes you keenly aware of what has to go where in order for the whole process to work. My knee bent forward yesterday pretty much on its own, without a lot of focused concentration on my part. That helps my foot to move forward without dragging on the floor (an important safety tip if you want to avoid tripping and falling!).

My foot isn't dragging so much anymore. That reminds me that it all started with my foot dragging on the floor a little...

May Day

No News is, Well, No News!

Jun 27, 2011 10:32pm

Went to a follow-up with the neuro-surgeon who saw me in the hospital right after the stroke. He was supposed to review the results of my last MRI done on 6/16. But, as we already knew, there was nothing new to report. After 3-1/2 weeks the blood had still not been reabsorbed and so they couldn't see anything else that might be lurking behind it (such as a tumor or some such thing). So, in this case, no news is no news. That means another MRI in a month and another follow-up appointment. In the meantime I'm supposed to visit my previous neurologist and my cardiac surgeon to see what they think.

Every day I get just a little bit better, even with walking with my Frankenstein's monster foot. Good thing too cuz this world is still not terribly wheelchair friendly! Wheelchairs don't do so well on gravel or curbs without cutouts or in tight places! So, the walker is the thing. Even that can be scary at times--and slow! When left to my own mobility getting to and fro can take forever which means having to build in extra "travel" time. We're also learning to send David--or whoever has the privilege of carting me around--ahead as a scout to see how wheelchair--or walker--friendly a destination might be and what the challenges and pitfalls might be.

Challenges abounded at the neuro-surgeon's office which is housed in a beautiful old early 20th century mansion on a tree-lined street in Everett. While it was charming it was a gimp's nightmare!

First of all, wheelchair traffic has to park and enter from the alley in the rear (a fact that you only discover once you are close enough to the front door to read the small print!). Once in back the parking lot is comprised of loose gravel and the concrete ramp is really only accessible from the parking space at one end which was already occupied. We opted for the walker and some fancy footwork that might have given my PT's and OT's apoplexy but we managed without a tumble. Then there were all the lovely faux oriental throw rugs that I had to maneuver over!

Once in the building we had to stop at the first level to fill out paperwork and then back into the elevator to get to the next level for the appointment. Good thing his group is moving to a new location cuz they obviously have grown too big for this historic monument so there are piles of things to have to scoot around with a walker. You get the general idea!

When we got home I met with the home care OT (Also named Chrystie (sounds like Christie)...is this a requirement for the job?!). I passed all her tests, including the Indian Princess sewing project! So that means she'll work with me! No, what it really means is that she has a pretty good idea of what I still need help with and we'll begin in earnest probably Thursday.

Now I'm exhausted after all the walking I did today so it's off to bed!

From the Going Green at the Beach Blog

Jun 28, 2011 11:47pm

Lots have been happening at the beach but recently we had a new opportunity to test out one of our green building schemes: universal design. The whole idea of universal design is that a home is built for life and built for anyone to live in. This means that the home will function well regardless of someone's physical capabilities. What makes this a green concept (even though it is not necessarily part of green building checklists) is the idea that the home is built for life or "aging in place." If we can build one home to last throughout a lifetime that eliminates the need to build many homes for many different stages of life, hence saving on materials, energy and environmental impacts.

May Day

At Going Green at the Beach we tried to incorporate some of these concepts at least on the main floor. Getting to the main floor is a challenge for the physically impaired but once inside the house much of the first floor is accessible by wheelchair and/or walker. I got to experience that first hand. And I didn't have to wait until I was "elderly." On May 23, at the ripe old age of 53, I suffered a hemorrhagic stroke which paralyzed my right foot, leg, arm and hand. After 3 days in CCU I was transferred to inpatient rehab for 3-1/2 weeks and discharged with a wheelchair, a walker and instructions for my family on how to help me get around, shower, dress, etc. I had made great progress in rehab but still needing to use DME (durable medical equipment).

How glad we were--and how impressed my therapists and doctors were--that we had made the decision to incorporate universal design concepts into our home. That meant there were very few changes that had to be made to accommodate my safe homecoming. We already had installed a Kohler shower with low threshold, built-in grab bars, built-in bench and hand-held shower head. Also, in the main floor bath we have a pedestal sink for easy access and enough room to turn a wheelchair around easily. We had also planned ahead during the framing stage to install a beam as a backer board so that installing a grab bar for the toilet was painless. If this had been a permanent situation (thankfully it appears not to be!) we would have also been able to easily install a pocket door between the bathroom and what was the office as we had also during framing installed the pocket door frame. Throughout the rest of the main living level we had, at our interior design consultant Keith Miller's advice, our light switches located lower so they are reachable at wheelchair height. The same is true of our Sharp microwave drawer which is located in the side of the kitchen island for access at a lower height. The office was quite easily converted to a bedroom for me and the extra-wide hidden doorway is helpful for wheelchair access. And of course, the use of only hard-surface flooring makes wheelchair and walker mobility much easier.

The things that we had to install after the fact: an additional handrail down the stairs from the street level to the front porch and the grab bar by the toilet. What we could have done differently?: Install those remote controlled switches for the ceiling fan/lights which I thought were unnecessary but now would really appreciate the ease of controlling my own fan/light and find a way to make the doorway to the bathroom wider (the wheelchair fits through but just barely) or pull-away hinges. Overall, the plan has worked well. Especially since we have help with the laundry which is on the second floor and inaccessible to me as yet!

(Learn more about Going Green at the Beach at www.goinggreenatthebeach.com and check out my CarePages photo album for pics of my rooms.)

"Going Green at the Beach"--for those who are unfamiliar—is the title we gave to our "green" house project. Our rebuild of a 100-year-old cabin on the beach became an educational event and made us celebrities for a brief period. I would tell you more about it here but then you wouldn't buy my next book which is a tell-all about the project. You'll just have to stay tuned.

What They Want to Hear

Jul 1, 2011 10:02am

Let's face it. I have always been the caretaker of other peoples' feelings. It is who I am. It is the role I have played my entire life. It is in my DNA. I'm not really sure where those genes came from as I don't particularly think my forebears exhibited the same traits based on my experiences of them. Perhaps I am some new strain, a mutant if you will (which is not necessarily a bad thing if the mutation makes the species more adaptable). Perhaps that is why is happened. I have not, in any way, shape, or form had a horrible life at all. But as in any life there have been ups and downs and disappointments. And my way of dealing with the times, good or bad, has frequently been to take care of the "other's" feelings. I was the spatula, smoothing out the spread. I am the consummate "mother."

As a result, I find myself throughout this current experience sometimes digging deep for good news and practically never sharing when I feel discouraged or disappointed or frustrated or impatient. Not that that happens a lot. But it happens. More often I find myself going along with what the "other" needs to hear--or believe--something really positive and/or significant. I'm not sure if it is because the "other" needs to have his/her own feelings bolstered. Maybe the "other" needs to think that I am doing well (whether or not that is true). Maybe the "other" clings to the commonly-held belief (thank you Norman Vincent Peale) that thinking positively is the only way to achieve healing. I think the ultimate reason is that the hard stuff is, well, hard to hear. And ultimately, no matter how much we try to fight against it--some more successfully than others--it is in our entire collective human DNA to be somewhat selfish, to do what is necessary to protect ourselves to survive. And part of that selfishness (translated "survival mode") comes through in needing our world--and everything and everyone in it--to be "good" (translated "healthy, happy, productive, __________"; fill in the blank).

I hope that you do not take this wrong. I have made amazing progress. I am light years ahead of where I was nearly 6 weeks ago and I am fully aware of this. I know that I am very "blessed" or "lucky," however you choose to "hold" it. Hemorrhagic strokes are associated with higher mortality rates according to what I have read. And when mine happened the neurosurgeon commented that he wasn't going to have to do surgery to stop the bleeding which was a good thing because my bleed was located in a nearly impossible-to-reach-place. I never lost the use of my hand completely and remarkably--and this has been called "rare" by more than one medical professional--my hand function has come back first and rather quickly. I never lost my speech, hearing, sight or memory functions. In the grand scheme of things I made out "like a bandit" on this one. And I am grateful.

But...I still have my down moments and my "gray" days. Mostly because I am impatient. And I'm feeling sorry for myself. I cooked dinner last night! By myself!! From start to finish! But I was exhausted afterward and frustrated with my limitations. I know, I know...but, you say, that is AMAZING!! That is so WONDERFUL!! And you are right. It's just that sometimes I want to wallow a bit. I want to be sad that I have plants that have died or are dying. I want to be sad that I had to give up spending the summer caring for my darling grandson. I want to be sad that I don't get to walk the beach or wear sandals! I know, I know...this is clearly just temporary. I will be back to "normal" soon and there will be other days, other seasons God willing.

And here I am...having talked myself out of feeling sorry for myself. The sun just came out.

I Got a Basket

Jul 5, 2011 4:15pm

So I started in-home therapy (no, NOT that kind!) last week and they are already talkin' about graduating me to "outpatient" which seems like an contradiction since it means I'll be going BACK to the hospital or clinic to continue my PT & OT. That means, technically I'll be more "in" than I am now...but anyways...that actually is progress. It means that I've proven that I can maneuver the steps to and from the front door well enough to do it on a regular basis by going somewhere else for my therapy. I am okay with this (although my chauffeurs may not be!) as it means I'll get to use more high-tech equipment than the elastic bands and my aluminum walker to keep getting better.

May Day

I'm SO ready too! This sittin' in a wheelchair and shuffling around with a walker is really crampin' my style! The weather is finally beautiful and I want to be out in the garden, walking the beach, and wearing FLIP FLOPS & SANDALS! (Not my lovely walking exercise shoes with the jogging socks and AFO!) Plus, I'm sure as heck not LOSING weight with all this sitting around! And I'm tired of feeling old and decrepit! A feeling that is exacerbated by my wardrobe, the fanny pack (or "butt" pack as my friend Pat--who loaned me hers cuz I wouldn't be caught dead ow[n]ing one![--calls it]) I am now consigned to wearing, and then, of course, the newest old-age accessory I received today: the basket for my walker! Gee whiz! Next it will be the horn! Why my family is oohing and ahhing over this contraption is beyond me! There are few things in life that define old age more than a walker WITH A BASKET!! That is nothing to ooh and ahh over! I think it should elicit politely-silent pity more than any other emotion! If they think all these "cool" pieces of DME are "the cat's meow" then they should try "walking in my shoes!"

Remember how I wrote about FT at the hospital (Food Therapy, designed to make you want to get better as quickly as possible so you could escape having to eat it??!)? Well, this is my new "disincentive": OAT (old-age therapy) designed to make you want to get better before you slide down the slippery slope toward appliquéd sweatshirts and dinner at 4 with a senior citizen discount! Ahhggghhhh!!!!!!

I Saw My Bedroom Today

Jul 7, 2011 12:28am

I woke up feeling pretty tired and sore and the last thing I wanted to do was...well...nothing. But I have learned that the best thing to do when I feel that way is to just get up and get going, which is tougher these days when just getting going is a struggle. But I did. I made my own breakfast, poured my own coffee, and got down to business at the *computer...only to find out that WAVE cable (which handles our cable, internet & phone line) was down! Cr*p! I could have done my arm exercises but I was too tired and sore. So I played "slug" for David while he went down to Bellevue to run an errand.*

When I got home my PT arrived. We started with my leg exercises which were excruciating (although I am slowly doing more of them myself). Then we did some standing leg exercises at the kitchen counter. It was not unlike standing at the "barre" in ballet although I was not nearly as graceful! And then she said, "Do you want to try the stairs?" So I did. I walked all the way up to the second floor! And then, David said, "Since you're here do you want to see your bedroom?" It was surreal! I walked into my bedroom for the first time in 6-1/2 weeks! It seems like an eternity and yet it seemed like no time had passed. I walked up and then I walked down. And now I will start looking into options for out-patient therapy. I have officially graduated.

I can tell you that it is a bit weird to be moving closer to being "normal" again. I have gotten so used to the new "normal," to knowing what to expect from my body "after." It really is like starting all over again and sometimes it is a bit frightening…

Sound the All Clear; It Was Only Gas!

Jul 8, 2011 9:57pm

It was May 1982, about 3 weeks before my due date with my first child. I suddenly started to, well, leak. It wasn't a lot but it concerned me. I had taken all the classes and read all the books and literature and listened to my OB. This could very likely be amniotic fluid. In other words, my "water" likely broke. I had learned that if this should happen I should get to hospital quickly (at least that was SOP in 1982). So we hopped in the car with my bag and raced (yes, we went over the 35 MPH speed limit!) across the tide flats from our home in Northeast Tacoma to St. Joseph's hospital's emergency room. After what seemed like hours (doesn't it always in the ER?) the verdict came down: "Sorry, Mrs. Porter. It wasn't amniotic fluid." (Translated: You must have wet your pants!) Major embarrassment for me and grief from my husband who somehow felt that he could share in my embarrassment (NOT!!). And, of course, he lost all confidence in me knowing when it was really "time" so that when I officially did go into labor 3 weeks later he wouldn't believe me! This time I swear he drove below the speed limit and when we got to the ER he kept telling everyone it was probably another false alarm, which we certainly wouldn't be staying!

Fast forward to July 7, 2011. I was laying peacefully on the sofa, reading a book, keeping my feet up fighting an onset of edema in my ankle and waiting for dinner to be ready. For the record: I had only eaten a benign piece of salmon with vegetables over greens for lunch and some pistachios for a snack several hours earlier (i.e. nothing spicy or greasy or otherwise capable of creating indigestion.); I was, I repeat, relaxed with nothing especially on my mind, lost in my book; in other words, I was minding my own business!

Suddenly around 7:30 I started having what I thought at first was heartburn (God know why!)_but this rapidly turned into excruciating pain like I have never felt before (except perhaps during labor). I tried to sit up; the pain was still as bad. I cried out in anguish (we're talking serious pain here!) and asked Kyle to get me some Tums. I chewed them as he helped me to my bed; maybe laying down would help. The pain got worse and nausea ensued. Kyle got a bowl in case I vomited. I rocked back and forth with my head in my arms over the bowl, wondering what to do when the cold sweating started. According to my family I went very pale then and I noticed both hands start to tingle and then go numb. Clearly this had to be more than a little indigestion!

We called 911 and our good friends at the fire station up the street came "running." By the time they arrived the pain was starting to subside. They ran an EKG which showed nothing unusual but decided it best to transport me back to Providence. All I could think of was the vision of my family's faces (David, Mattie, Kyle, LeAnne Carl) filled with anguish! This was all they needed! (It reminded me of the funny book I've been reading by Suzy Becker, "I had Brain Surgery, What's Your Excuse?" in which she humorously illustrates the toll her health was taking on everyone else by drawing a cartoon of a toll booth with a sign that reads "Stop and Pay Toll: Diet, Sleep, Aging, Income, Smoking, Vacation." In Carl & LeeAnne's case it could have included "the ability to ever go back home!") I really wasn't worried about me. I became pretty convinced by then that this was probably not angina.

At ER they ran their EKG's and did an enzyme blood test. Nothing. Still should keep me over night for "observation." "Could it be indigestion?" "Have you ever had a panic or anxiety attack?" Another blood enzyme test 4 hours later. Nothing. Another one 2 hours later. Nothing. In the morning I went for a CT and stress tests. Nothing. Diagnosis? "We're not sure; could have been GERD (Gastroesophageal reflux disease)." (Translated: "Gas"). "Avoid spicy or greasy food and we could also prescribe something like "Protonix©." "I'm already taking Protonix©. Have been since I went the hospital last time." "Oh...well, maybe you need to up the dosage for a week or so."

The nurse came in with my discharge papers. "So, you know, these were very good tests that they ran but they are still not 100% accurate. You should be mindful of severe chest pain, cold sweats..." "I had those!" "Oh, well, what I'm saying is that you just can't be sure so if that happens again you should call 911." Great. So they can run another bunch of tests to tell me that I'm full of...

So I left with another folder, another set of discharge papers, another list of my prescriptions, another travel size hand sanitizer. I passed on another pair of "gripper" socks or another hospital-issue water bottle. And I left more pride behind...

It's a Bird! It's a Plane! It's...SuperBug!

Jul 10, 2011 10:21am

When the events of Thursday, July 7 began to occur my loving family gathered around me, wringing their hands and asking me one the following questions (in a variety of forms) repeatedly: "What do you think it could be?" or "Do you think this could have been caused by ________?" (you fill in the blank.) After the umpteenth time of being asked what I thought it could be I wanted to yell out "I don't know!!!" (Hey, did you notice that I can add emphasis to my CarePages posts now? Yeah! Out of the blue they added "font style, lists, and alignment"! So now I can use bold, italic, or underlining, for emphasis instead of just converting to ALL CAPS, which is really the accepted – not--form of written yelling at someone. It appears that they might not have worked out all the bugs yet, as "font name and size, font color and background color are there but most of the time appear in "grayed" form which means you can't access them and you can't use keyboard shortcuts to change from plain to bold to back again. You have to scroll back up the page and use the mouse the click on the icon. The "style' option is definitely a big step forward for those of us who like to use emphasis in our writing though. But I digress...)

Speaking of "bugs," I'm pretty sure I've figured out what was wrong! Now before you accuse me of erring by self-diagnosing (Oh sure. Now it's not acceptable although last Thursday night my family expected it!) I will be seeing my own GP, along with a series of other doctors this week (added to the cadre I saw Thursday and Friday) but to my credit I have taken all your suggestions and experiences to heart and have investigated them online, comparing the accepted symptoms to mine and have come to a conclusion: it's some sort of bug. I know, I know, it doesn't sound nearly as critical or dramatic to call it a "bug" but that seems to be the most plausible answer. Herewith are some of your fine suggestions and why they were dismissed: (and now I will use my new "lists" tool!)

Pancreatitis: (funny, CarePages editor, which deals I think with mostly health-related issues doesn't have "pancreatitis" in it's text dictionary! But it doesn't have "CarePages" either...But I digress again...) from the government Web site (which I would think is more trustworthy than, say, WebMD) Symptoms may include: Abdominal pain: Check, Definitely had that!; Chills: Didn't have those; Clammy skin: Check, definitely had that; Fatty stools: Don't mean to reveal too much here but no; Fever: No; Mild jaundice: No (family just reported I was very pale); Nausea: Yes; Sweating: And how!; Weakness: Could have been caused by a number of things, not the least of which was fighting excruciating pain so I would vote no; Weight loss: I wish! (emphasis definitely and purposefully added!);Vomiting: again, might be TMI (ask your local teen for definition!) but only felt slightly like I might...Final analysis: No. Not enough positive evidence to support.

Gall Bladder/Gall stones, from the Univ. of Maryland Medical Center (I resisted checking the drhoffman.com Web site; didn't really seem as credible.): The primary symptom [of biliary pain or colic--look it up yourself! or inflammation] is typically a steady gripping or gnawing pain in the upper right abdomen near the rib cage I think I can rule this out right away. What's happening to me is definitely happening around the center to left of my abdomen and the stomach is definitely involved. Complaints of gas, nausea, and abdominal discomfort after meals [additional symptoms of acute inflammation] Mine definitely did not happen after a meal.[Symptoms of gall stones] Jaundice (yellowish skin); Dark urine, lighter stools, or both; Rapid heartbeat and abrupt blood pressure drop; Fever, chills, nausea and vomiting, and severe pain in the upper right abdomen. Again, not enough match mine. Final analysis: No. Not enough positive evidence to support.

May Day

Something I ate (i.e. too spicy, too greasy, just plain bad), from the annals of Anna Porter's experience (seems credible enough): reaction to type of food such as spicy or greasy, generally gas bloating, maybe heartburn.............definitely not. hadn't eaten in several hours and the last thing I ate was baked salmon over fresh lettuce. Hardly a candidate for spicy or greasy. Reaction to bad food such as potato salad that has been out too long or restaurant salad bars or fish that smells bad, generally stomach pain accompanied by vomiting and/or diarrhea .....again, definitely not. The salmon was most fresh, as was my lettuce, and did not smell bad or funny. And, I did not have those kinds of symptoms. Final analysis: No. Did not fit either description.

Irritable Bowel Syndrome, from the Mayo Clinic Web site (can't get much more reliable than that!) and conversations with my dear sister and sister-in-law who both suffer from the disease: Abdominal pain or cramping...definitely upper pain; cramping? maybe not. A bloated feeling... not at the time, some time later for sure. Gas (flatulence)...nope. Diarrhea or constipation – sometimes alternating bouts of constipation and diarrhea...again, nope, not at the time but the "d" word followed the next day. Sorry again for TMI! Mucus in the stool...okay, yes again. Final analysis: Inconclusive. Possibly so...But what about the upper left unbearable pain, the sweating nausea and the sudden numbness tingling in my hands???

So what then? It certainly, within a 95% certainty, wasn't my heart.

Then, last night my friend Sylvia came to visit. She sat beside me and began to talk in those quiet, almost conspiratorial tones, "Where was your pain again? What did it feel like? I had the same thing last week. It was horrible!" "Like giving birth?" "Yes! Definitely!" And then we went on to compare other symptoms which were incredibly alike! So could we both be suffering from the same pancreatitis or gall bladder disease? Not likely! More likely, we determined that "where two or more are gathered" and have similar symptoms in or around the same time the culprit was most likely contagious! In other words, in the common vernacular, our common ailments were caused by a bug. Now, as I said, I will be poked and prodded by other more credible diagnosticians this week, but for now I am content with the self-diagnosis. Thanks for all your suggestions!

Dr? Dr. Dr? Dr. Dr? Dr...

Jul 14, 2011 11:28pm

So how many of you got the obscure reference to the Chevy Chase/Dan Akroyd movie "Spies Like Us"? Anyway...this pretty much describes my week and why I have been somewhat silent for a few days. Tuesday my chauffeur (brother-in-law Carl) shuffled me off to Seattle to the UW Med Center for my follow-up appointment with my neurologist. There I got to bring her PA up to date on my entire life (or so it's beginning to seem!) from the first TIA episode through the fall that banged up my head to the stroke. We talked about the PFO study and the neurosurgeon's thoughts about resolving it. Then we looked at the pictures from my last MRI. In those we were able to see 1 big white fluffy-looking blob and 2 smaller nondescript gray blobs. According to the PA the white blob is where my last stroke occurred and where the blood is apparently still stubbornly pooled masking who-knows-what behind it. The two gray blobs are "dead zones" (my term), places where there "isn't anything" as she put it, indicating most likely a stroke occurred there. These supposed strokes happened without my knowledge, which is a bit alarming but not infrequent. It is the fact that I've had, now, apparently 4 strokes in as many years that encouraged the neurosurgeon to press me to investigate the PFO closure again.

After our discussion, the PA went out to consult with the DR who decided she wants me to see, you guessed it! Another doctor! This one is at Harborview Medical Center and is "the stroke neurologist" in Seattle. Then I was shipped over to the lab where they removed about 2 quarts of blood for "some tests"!

May Day

On Wednesday, Carl took me to Bellevue for my follow-up with my GP and my belated physical (as if I haven't been poked, prodded, folded and mutilated enough by the medical community!). She pronounced me looking and seeming to be much better, took some more blood and tests, wrote-off my recent emergency room visit as most likely belated food poisoning and sent me on my way.

Today we trekked back to UWMC for my appointment with my cardiologist. He is the one I saw after my TIA and the PFO study and we decided to put off any procedure. This time he wanted to defer to my neurologists. The neurosurgeon seemed very gung-ho about it. The neurologist wanted a second (or third?) opinion. It appears that this decision hinges on what the "super-stroke" neurologist has to say and we're still waiting to have an appointment with him.

In the afternoon we went back down to Providence Everett for my fourth MRI. The hope is that this one will show that the blood has been reabsorbed, revealing a possible cause of the brain bleed. Not sure when I'll get to schmooze with the neurosurgeon on those results. Hopefully next week. In other words, we're playing the waiting game. In the meantime...I am getting better ever so slowly! I actually moved my right toes the other night (if anyone had ever told me that I would be blogging about the most mundane, ordinary physical activities as something monumental I would have thought he/she was crazy!! I mean...did you ever think you'd be hanging on every word as someone described in detail the movements of her appendages??!! or for that matter, her doctor visits??!!). I also (now don't tell my PT's OT's about this!) have walked a bit in the house without my walker!! I can tell that my leg and foot are coming around and it can't happen soon enough! I mean, Sophie is pulling herself up to standing and Jackie is close behind! I gotta get a move on if I'm gonna beat them to the punch!

Thank you dear friends for your continued loving messages of support, calls, prayers, thoughts and interest! You're the best!

The What Ifs

Jul 17, 2011 11:21pm

I believe that everyone who goes through some traumatic experience and survives asks this same question: "What if...?" God knows why we do this, as if the experience itself were not enough; somehow we have to play through all the other possible scenarios, usually scarier ones. I wonder if that is something like people gawking at an accident. Or how characters in a scary movie always need to look behind the dark door or walk down the dark hallway, as if they just have to check things out no matter what the risk?

I have had my share of what-if's with this most recent experience. Some of my what-ifs relate to the other possible scenarios with a not-so-happy ending. I wonder: What if I had been on the road when this happened, miles from any medical facility? What if the hemorrhaging hadn't stopped on its own? What if the statistics of higher mortality rates with this type of stroke had applied to me? I also wonder a different sort of what if: What if my leg and/or foot don't fully recover? It could happen. I was told that usually the arm and hand come back last and that many patients never regain the full use of their hands. What if, in my case, it is the foot and leg? We don't want to, but we need to think about these what-ifs, these potentialities. Not that we want to allow negative thinking to rule our behaviors, but realistic thinking is really the prudent thing to do. I know I'm growing impatient with my foot and leg; I know it could still take some time and that I am making some progress. But what if???

Medical Mayhem

Jul 22, 2011 2:25pm

And now, a microscope into the maze of medicine wherein "coordinated medical care" does not really exist and the patient is left holding the (medical) bag...And you have to laugh or else you'd cry or scream! (Note: Names have been changed to protect the guilty!)

Nut-rition[32] *Director: You've been placed on a "cardiac diet." Do you understand what that entails?*

Me (to myself): Yes, no fat, no salt, no flavor! But I had a hemorrhagic stroke that was supposedly not caused by high blood pressure. So exactly why am I on a cardiac diet? (to Nut-rition Director) Yes, I understand.

Nut-rition Director: Here are some helpful tips on eating healthier (translated: patients only end up here, with stroke, because of their unhealthy habits: smoking, not exercising, and eating poorly. You probably fit into one or more of those categories but I'm too much of an automaton to get to know you and your habits first. I just pass out these meaningless Xeroxed eating tips.) Do you have any questions?

Me: Yes...when will I start getting the whole grains, legumes, and fresh vegetables that are recommended on this sheet?

Nut-rition Director: Oh, you can order any of those things for your meals! (translated: that is if by "whole grains" you mean "brown white cardboard bread," by "legumes" you mean "peanut butter," and by "fresh vegetables" you mean "the white parts of the iceberg lettuce, one slice of slightly frozen/defrosted cucumber and a chunk of taste-less tomato imported from Chile")

Me: Honey? Could you bring in some good food for dinner tonite?

Me (to Dr. Rehab): Since you have moved my discharge from 6/14 to 6/17 how will you handle getting me to my MRI appointment and

---

[32] Purposely spelled wrong to emphasize the "Nut-tiness" of her job! It sure wasn't the *nutrition* I'm sure she studied to practice.

follow-up with Dr. Headcut (neurosurgeon in their hospital system!) on 6/16?

Dr. Rehab: I don't know. We don't know anything about that. It would have to take place after you are discharged. You'll have to re-schedule. (after some more conversation) Okay, I'll call and see what Dr. Headcut wants to do...(some time passes; we get to the day of the MRI) Okay. We're going to get you into our MRI facility this morning. Not sure what time. They will come and get you. Then we have rescheduled your appointment with Dr. Headcut to 6/27.

Dr. Rehab: Okay. Upon 4 weeks (aka 7/15) after discharge from inpatient care, please make an appointment to see the physiatrist.

Me (to myself): whatever that is! I mean, spell check doesn't even recognize the term! And neither do any of the other medical professionals I mention the term to! And, in fact, if I am to believe Richard Staehler, MD at www.spine-health.com that is the correct spelling and yet, it was spelled "physiotry" on my discharge papers!

Dr. Rehab (again): He will continue to monitor your progress and your medications.

Me: Hello? I need to make an appointment with Dr. Physiatry. (pause) Not until 7/27? (aka 5-1/2 weeks after discharge!) Okay (feebly).

Inpatient Rehab Coordinator: Okay. We have sent your discharge information and recommendation to Home Health Rehab. They should be calling you early next week to schedule. If you don't hear from them, call this number. (translated: You won't hear from them. You'll need to call)

Me: (to Home Health Rehab): Hello? This is Anna Porter. I was referred to HHR last week. Can you tell me the status? (pause) I should be hearing from them by this coming Friday or next week at the latest? (translated: HHR didn't finally begin for another week and a half.)

Neurosurgeon, Dr. Headcut: We can't come to any conclusions on what might have caused this but since you've had multiple events and this confirmed PFO, I think you should follow-up with your cardiologist and neurologist and pursue the PFO repair.

Neurosurgeon's Asst.: I'll be happy to call to make those appointments.

Me: You'll probably have better luck so please do.

Neurosurgeon's Asst.: (into phone) Hello? Yes, this is Dr. Headcut's office calling. We have a mutual patient who suffered a stroke and we'd like you to do a follow-up. (pause) Not until late August? Are you sure? (pause) Can you put her on the cancel call list? (pause) Really? Alright, please put her down for that appointment. (into phone) Hello? Yes, this is Dr. Headcut's office calling. We have a mutual patient who suffered a stroke and we'd like you to do a follow-up. (pause) I see. So since it has been more than 3 years since she has seen the Dr. we have to get the Dr.'s permission to make an appointment? (pause) Fine. We'll get the necessary paperwork off. (to me) I'll ask Dr. Headcut to call directly.

Me: (having found the email address for my neurologist) Dear Dr. Headtreat. I recently had another stroke......was wondering if you could expedite getting me in to see you and Dr. Heart?

Dr. Headtreat: (via email) So sorry to hear this happened again. My office will call and schedule you for next week. Dr. Heart? Can you please schedule Anna to see you as well? (score one for patient-pull over Dr.-Dr. courtesy!)

Dr. PCP (primary care physician): I'm glad you're doing better. I really want to up your blood pressure meds; it's still higher than I'd like to see it. (translated: probably caused your stroke). And I'd like to get you back on a statin (cholesterol med). I'd be very interested in hearing what the cardiologist recommends (translated: this has nothing to do with your stroke but I'm overly concerned with your cholesterol and blood pressure!) See you in about 3 weeks to follow up.

Dr. Headtreat's PA (because Dr. Headtreat didn't have time to see me directly but scheduled my appointment on a day that she was available for consult): Well, after all you have told me, I'm thinking that Dr. Headcut might be right. But let me consult with Dr. Headtreat first. I'll be right back. (time passes; I read my book) Okay, Dr. Headtreat really feels that before Dr. Heart does anything about the PFO that you should see Dr. Strokeheadtreat at Harborview. She is the best at stroke neurology. (translated: you have a better chance of being struck by lightning than getting in to see her in this century.) Our office will refer you and you'll hear from them.

Dr. Heart: Good to see you again. I'm sorry you had another "incident." (because, just as in "Harry Potter" we dare not speak the name for fear of giving it credence and conjuring it up again!). I understand that Dr. Headtreat's office is trying to get you into see Dr. Strokeheadtreat. I really don't want to make the decision to proceed with the PFO repair until she weighs in. As far as statin drugs, fish oil, etc. I'm not convinced that these are necessary or prudent. I mean, your cholesterol is higher than normal but not terribly high and the studies don't go out that far. I mean, we know about the affects after 5 years of use but not after 20 years of use. I say we wait.

Me (to myself): Uh-oh. Dr. PCP isn't gonna like hearing this. You tell her!

Dr. Heart: I'll send over my notes/recommendations to Dr. PCP.HHR PT,

May Day

Nurse OT: Okay. We're discharging you. We feel that you are ready for outpatient therapy at the facility of your choice. (Have a nice life!)

Me (to myself): Where does that leave me? Hmmm...

Me, after some time of silence on the whole physical therapy thing has past: Hello, Outpatient Therapy? I've been discharged from HHR. I'd like to schedule my outpatient therapy now. (pause) I see. Who would provide you with those orders/prescription? (no clue) I see.

Me: Hello, Inpatient Therapy? I've been discharged from HHR. Can you ask Dr. Rehab about getting me assigned to outpatient therapy? Thank you.

(ring, ring) Me: Hello? Inpatient Therapy? Dr. Rehab can't help me? Once I've been discharged my PCP has to take over? (to myself: Are you kidding? My PCP doesn't know anything about any of this stuff!) Okay.

Me: Hello? Dr. PCP's office? I've been discharged from HHR. I'm supposed to start outpatient therapy. You're supposed to send orders. (pause during which it becomes abundantly clear that I was right; they're clueless!) I don't know how this works. I was just told your office was supposed to handle it. (pause) Okay. I need to call HHR and ask them to send information over? Okay.

Me: Hello? HHR? I'm trying to schedule my outpatient therapy (to myself: and why am I trying to schedule this? Aren't you all supposed to follow-through on this stuff???). Yes. I talked to Dr. Rehab. He discharged me (aka: washed his hands of me!). Can you send information to my PCP? Thank you.

Dr. PCP: Good to see you again. You look great! How are you feeling? So, did you see Dr. Heart? (translated: I haven't gotten a report back from him). Let's do some more blood tests. Everything else looks great. That little "incident" (aka: the one that landed you in emergency again!) was most likely food poisoning. And now your colon is upset. Yes, that's the pain you feel in your groin.

Me (to myself as I'm being dismissed by Dr. PCP): But that pain has been there for a few weeks before the "incident"....

Me: Hmmmm...I've run out of the vitamins and the indigestion meds prescribed by Dr. Rehab and am about to run out of the "anti-tone" medicine. What to do since I'll be out of those before I see Dr. Physiatry? I'll try calling the pharmacy and put it in their hands...

(time goes by...) Me: Hello? Inpatient Therapy? Could you ask Dr. Rehab what I should do about running out of my meds before I see Dr. Physiatry?

Inpatient Rehab: I checked with Dr. Rehab. He says that since he discharged you...

Me (to myself): Oh yeah. I remember. He has washed his hands of me...Me: So what do I do now?

Inpatient Rehab: Dr. Rehab says to call your PCP.

Me (to myself): Oh yeah...like that's gonna work!!

Me: Dr. PCP's office? Yes, just checking. Did you get the paperwork from HHR? No? Okay. I'll call them again. Also, I'm running out of my "anti-tone" medicine...yes, it's spelled B-a-c-l-o-f-e-n. Have the pharmacy fax the refill request to you? But will they do that since Dr. PCP wasn't the prescribing Dr.? (pause...Dr. PCP's receptionist is stymied). Okay. I'll try.

Me: Pharmacist? So here's the deal on my "anti-tone" medicine...(I tell the whole story again!) So can you fax the refill request to my PCP? (pause...Pharmacist is stymied...I mean really, in the history of modern medicine am I the first patient they have dealt with who has run into this problem of being in the medical care cracks?!) Okay. Thank you for following up.

Me: HHR? Did you send my discharge papers to my PCP? (pause) Okay. Thank you for faxing those over right away.

Me: Dr. PCP's office? Did you get the refill request? Did you send it back to the pharmacy? Thank you. Did you get the discharge papers? Well, as I understand it you would now send orders to Providence Outpatient Rehab so that I can continue my therapy (To myself: by now I am thinking the only therapy I need is mental!!). Okay. Thank you. (to be continued...)

Medical Mayhem, cont.

Jul 22, 2011 2:46pm

Dr. Strokeheadtreat's office: Hi. This is Dr. Strokeheadtreat's assistant. I understand that you have been referred to our office by Dr. Headtreat. Unfortunately, the earliest I could get you in is mid-November.

Me (feebly): Umm...is that the best you can do? I don't know that Dr. Headtreat will want to wait that long...

Dr. Strokeheadtreat' asst: Well, I could get you in sooner to see Dr. Ijustgotmydegree. He would be in consultation with Dr. Strokeheadtreat.

Me: Hmmm...Let me see what Dr. Headtreat says.

Me via email to Dr. Headtreat and Dr. Heart: Dr. Strokeheadtreat can't see me until November. What would you like to do? (translated: why don't you try throwing your professional weight around and see if you can do better, especially since my good insurance is running out at the end of September and then I get to start all over again with a new insurance company and a ridiculously high deductible!)

Dr. Headtreat: I'll contact her office.

(ring, ring)

Dr. Strokeheadtreat' asst: Hi, I can get you in to see Dr. I'mjustalameassassociateofDrSuperstrokeheadtreats's on August 10. Alright?

Me: That would be fine (I guess).

HHR: Hi, this is your HHR PT. So we got a call from your PCP's office. They need to know where you've decided to continue your therapy

(Me to myself: oh, I don't know...probably Western State Hospital at this point!!). They were under the impression that you wanted to continue at Providence but I thought you said that was too far away.

Me (to myself): I never said that! My family might have but I didn't...At any rate, I already told the PCP's office to send them to Providence so why the questions??)

Me: No, Providence is my choice.

HHR: Okay. I'll get back to the PCP. (translated: good luck getting into Outpatient therapy any time soon!!

Me via email: Dr Heart, did you send your opinions to my PCP?

Dr. Heart: I'm gone for the weekend but will check my records on Monday.

May Day

Me (to myself): It's okay...I already know the answer. Would you please send them when you get back??

Me to my friend-who-works-on-claims-for-a-large-insurance-provider: You would not believe the run-around I have been through and how much of this stuff I have had to figure out on my own through multiple phone calls!!

My friend: Funny you should mention that. We had a staff meeting yesterday where we heard that our company is working on a pilot program where our RNs on staff would actually be assigned to patients and would be responsible for handling all of these connections for the patient.

*Me: You mean like a case manager? What a novel idea!! (to myself: It's about **** time!! Now if other insurance companies would follow suit...)*

Little Miss Independent

Jul 29, 2011 10:51am

Carl & LeAnne left on Tuesday morning to go home. For the most part, for good. It was a bittersweet farewell...they have been the pillars that have held my family up during my long "absence." They have made sure that everyone was nourished--physically and emotionally, especially David. They have washed clothes, grocery-shopped, watered plants, cleaned floors, cooked meals, driven me to appointments, run errands, completed little "honey-do" tasks around the house and kept us company. While we have needed--and been grateful to--them so much there had to come a time when the baby birds left the nest. We had to fly on our own. And they needed to get home and get their lives back to normal. And we had to figure out new ways of surviving.

This passage leads to the next phase of FT (Family Therapy). I have to say that it is working! It's not that my family doesn't chip in but the way it works here is that they don't always (who am I kidding??! EVER!) see what needs to be done and do it. They need to be asked...sometimes cajoled...sometimes nagged to do those things. And I'm so used to just doing things to avoid the stress of trying to engage them. Plus, I like things a certain way and even though I have gotten really good (I think!) at letting go a bit more, I still think a kitchen floor should be washed more often than every other week when our house cleaner comes! FT, like OT (as my OT, Christie often reminded me) is geared toward making the patient more independent and literally working the therapist out of a job. (As you increase, I decrease). My family has subscribed to this way of thinking much more easily and readily than one might expect! And it is working!

I have now graduated to at least sweeping and mopping the kitchen and main floor bathroom floors. I empty and fill the dishwashers and wash the hand-washables. I cook dinner (have done complete meals by myself). I set the table, do some dusting, straighten out drawers, clean out the refrigerator...anything that I can do on the main floor. I have also learned to walk small distances without the walker (as long as I have something sturdy close by to grab as needed).

There are still too many things that I cannot do (laundry, gardening, walking the dog, grocery shopping...) for which I must count on my family. This forces me to do that which I usually avoid at all cost--ask. Please don't think that my family is uncaring. They care very much. But it just doesn't occur to them that these things don't take care of themselves. And they have stepped up when asked. And that is all part of the therapy. Whether they know it or not!

Just a Quickie!

Aug 6, 2011 12:44pm

I know you all might be wondering what happened to me but wanted you to know that I'm still here and not much has changed! I did go see the "physiatrist" on July 27. This was a follow-up on my physical therapy and meds prescribed while at Inpatient PT. He was a lovely man: kind, gentle, attentive. And I knew that he would set things straight with the whole Outpatient PT thing (which he did, immediately!). What I did not expect was that at the end of our visit he asked if I had any more questions. Then he asked if he could pray for me. "Of course" was my response. Then he asked if he could pray in the name of Jesus. "Of course" again was my response. Then he took my hands in his and spoke a prayer of such sweetness, comfort, joy, and caring that I have ever heard. It was heartfelt and beautiful and spoken as if we were old friends. There was nothing "fundamentalist" about it; nothing dramatic or charismatic. It was simple, pure and real. I wish that I had recorded it. I tried very hard to remember phrases but I can't. But I remember the moment.

The same day, at about the same time, my darling youngest son, Scot, out of the blue "texted" this note to me:

"I just wanted to say that im [sic] so happy, thankful, and proud that you guys are my parents. I love y'all very much, hope you're having a good day."

Thank you Scot. It was a good day indeed...

Taking Back My Life

Aug 9, 2011 10:39am

Last night we had a meeting, my darling husband and I. He had called for it by way of an Outlook calendar invitation and had asked me to prepare for it by considering this topic: "discuss taking our life (lives) back." I knew what he meant. Our collective lives--but especially his right now which is in major upheaval trying to juggle 2 jobs and the weight of supporting the household--seem "out of control" and being good corporate citizens of the human race, we feel that it is not only prudent – and our God-given right – but necessary to get back in control.

But the longer I pondered that notion the more bizarre it seemed to me. And a myriad of thoughts descended – none of which was exactly what he had in mind (and I'm sure he got more esoteric answers than he had hoped for).

What did it mean, "taking back my life"? My first thought was: "who said it was taken in the first place?" It reminded me of pondering a similar idea, "When I get my life back I will ____________ (fill in the blank). I have thought about that a lot. But the reality is, I have "had" (i.e. been living) my life all this time. This period is in fact "part of my life" and although it is not one of my favorite times, it is still my life. My life in not on "pause," I am not "away" or "busy," – like it or not, this IS my life, the same one I have always had just another chapter in it.

Okay, so I'll play along. As we talked David shared what motivated his meeting topic, which I fully understood. But I wasn't content to stick to the script (frustrating for him, I'm sure!) so next I ventured into another alternative thought: "taking our lives back (i.e. regaining some control of them) presumes that we have any control at all. This one hits home for me as well.

Now, those who truly believe in such things as karma, Zen and self-fulfilling prophecy might argue differently. They might say that everything that "happens" to us we brought upon ourselves, maybe even intentionally. I'm not quite there in my thinking. Maybe I DID bring on this stroke but not without supposedly trying to avoid it through the advice of modern Western medicine. 90% of hemorrhagic strokes are caused by high blood pressure. I was being treated for "high" blood pressure (we're talking merely 145/90 being my typical "high") and I had a hemorrhagic stroke. My doctors all concur that we "don't yet know what caused it." Not one of them has suggested that I planned or willed this on myself. That is even too esoteric for me to accept!

May Day

I am still of the mind that there are "outside sources" over which we have at least no "perceived" control: world economies, forces of nature, freewill of other human beings to take actions against us, etc. What I am getting at is that there seems to be so much that we just don't have control over and so the idea of taking control and taking our lives back seems ludicrous at best, hubris at worst. As if...

Maybe this wouldn't happen to everyone but going through this experience has left me with a different lens with which to view the world and life (ya think??!!). I can't help it. I have begun to look at the things that we all take for granted – physical abilities, platitudes and attitudes – differently. Everything is not black and white or easily explained away or overcome. Maybe coming to those revelations alone constitutes "taking back my life."

Hello? Dr. House?

Aug 17, 2011 8:28am

I know, I know...I owe you an update! Most of the time not much is happening these days, at least much that's monumental so that when there is something to report it seems like I should pounce on it! But life (aka work) keeps getting in the way! (oh, how I long for those halcyon days in the hospital when I had no cares...no, no! that's not right!).

So, herewith is the latest. Last Wednesday I finally had my appointment with Dr. Strokehead. I like Dr. S. He's very professional but very personable (why should we be surprised by that combo?) And he – unlike me – has an amazing memory. When he came into the exam room and sat down to discuss my case he said he remembered me.

Me (to myself): You remember me? How is that? We just met!

He (in response to my puzzled look): You came to see me in 2006 after your TIA.

Me: I did? Gee, I don't remember that! (to myself: Great! I really AM losing my mind! I don't remember him AT ALL!)

Anyway, he had looked over my records the day before (Really? You mean I don't have to tell you my whole life story all over again? How refreshing and...unusual!), had remembered my TIA, and had also reviewed my old slides and my new ones. He did ask me a few questions but then he turned to the computer. I mentioned that I had been told that I had had a couple other strokes (of which I had been unaware) and he started pouring back over the MRI's.

"Hmmmm," he said, "that's interesting." These are words, coming from your stroke neurologist, that are not exactly pleasing. "Interesting" to him could be "bad news" to me! Then he announced that it looked as though the "event" in 2006 showed in approximately the same area as the "event" in 2011. No one had seemed to notice that before. (??!!)

Me (to myself): That seems like a pretty big deal! I mean, how could all the radiologists and neurologists who had been looking at those things not have noticed that before this?? I guess that is kinda "interesting" as you call it.

He invited me to peer into the computer screen with him and showed me what he had found. I'm no doctor but he seemed to be on to something: there was a little white oval in my brain scan from 2006 and in about the same place, a slightly bigger white oval in my 2011 scan. Hmmm...that is indeed interesting...

But I quickly learned that "interesting" in this case did not translate into "aha!" or "eureka!" It was more like "huh! I wonder what that means!" I mean, I thought he would immediately launch into "Okay, so here's what happened and here's why and here's what we'll do."

May Day

Instead, I began to feel as though I had slipped through the TV screen into my own episode of "House"! He started speculating out loud. "I wonder what that means. Could it be that the two are somehow tied together? But why did the bleed happen? Is it some sort of infection? Or maybe your blood is hypercoagulable? Or..." He was clearly stumped! This is not what the patient wants to hear! I was wishing the rest of his young, brilliant, brash personal staff of doctors would show up so they could start speculating together and maybe come up with something...quick, like in the next 43 TV minutes! Where were they? And, BTW, why was I the one who was walking with a limp??!

Over the months I had resigned myself to accept my usual fate: I had a hemorrhagic stroke and they didn't know what had caused it (translated: we don't know how to prevent it from happening again). I could somehow live with that. I frequently had over the years. But finding "something" and not knowing what to make of it...that was unexpected and a bit unnerving!

He didn't seem unnerved! He seemed even...giddy! But not sure how to proceed. Then he formulated a plan (and even wrote it all down with numbered bullet points for me! I know! What a concept!):

First, perform a cerebral angiogram (yes, a CEREBRAL one. This one sends the little apparatus up through your, um, groin by way of an artery past your heart and up into the brain stem to deposit a little dye) to take a closer look (this is apparently an option that he and I discussed in 2006--okay, I'll take his word for it!--but decided against as it was a bit invasive and perhaps not necessary);

Second, to perform a lumbar puncture (spinal tap) to ascertain if there was some exotic infection going on;

Third, to run some blood work (aka donate a quart! It's never good when the nurse comes in to extract your blood and keeps exclaiming about--and apologizing for! – taking SO MUCH BLOOD!) to rule out hypercoaguability; and

Fourth, to "PRESENT CASE @ STROKE CONFERENCE" ...What??! I'm such an anomaly that you're taking this to the next medical conference??? I had flash backs to an appointment with Mattie's flustered neurologist who asked if it would be okay for her to present Mattie's tumor case--and write it up--at the next international neurology conference, aka Freak Show of Neurological Wonders. Turns out, as you will see later, that "conference" is a fancy term for "regularly-held meeting of local neurologists and radiologists to discuss 'neurological wonders' and take a vote on what to do next."

So he sent me off with assurances that I would hear from his assistant who would schedule all the procedures and then I would see him again in 2 months.

(Me, to myself: TWO MONTHS???!! I have to wait two more months?!) So, I dutifully donated my quart of blood and left.

(to be continued...)

Acronym Soup

Aug 17, 2011 9:22am

So, as I mentioned in the last episode, I left Dr. "House's", office expecting to hear from his assistant in a couple of days and looking forward to more poking and probing. NOT! What I didn't expect was to get a phone call on Friday evening at about 6:00 p.m. from...Dr. S! The stroke conference had met that afternoon and he wanted to get back to me right away.

(Me, to myself: uh, oh. don't like the sounds of this.)

He continued, giddy again (and man, can that guy talk!!): "But it's actually pretty good news!"

(Me, to myself: okay. that's better).

Then he began throwing the acronyms out. Turns out the group took a vote and decided that I have a "cerebral cavernous malformation," a CCM. These things are actually genetic. You were probably born with it. They were pretty sure that it wasn't an AVM (which is "badder" news?) and that in 2006 I had a DVM (no, not a doctor of veterinary medicine! although when I went to do research on the internet later I couldn't find any DVM that wasn't a doctor of veterinary medicine...turns out later I found that it was actually a developmental venous anomaly, or DVA!) but this time I had a CCM but that's interesting, usually if there is a CCM it would show up with a DVA but they hadn't seen the CCM in the 2006 slide, only a DVA, and he was going to have to ask into that, but at least it wasn't an AVM, so that meant I didn't have to have the cerebral angiogram since that wasn't necessary to diagnose the CCM and half the group decided that was the case (including Dr. S) but the other half of the group, including the Head of Neurology (Me to myself: isn't that funny? "Head" of "Neurology"?!), felt that they should go ahead with the angiogram to rule out an AVM, but he had wanted to call me right away mostly to let me know that there was a change in his plan and that we didn't now need to do the lumbar puncture, and the blood tests came back normal, and they weren't going to do the angiogram, although maybe, now that we were discussing it he was beginning to wonder if the other half of the group was right and they should do the angiogram to rule out an AVM and BTW you're right, I had forgotten to bring up the fact that after nearly 3 months the blood had not been reabsorbed, I wonder what that means? Maybe the cavernous malformation was oozing? Hmm, I'll have to talk some more with the radiologists to see what they think about that. But this is good news!

(Me to myself: I frankly don't see how! So I have a cavern in my head!) To Dr. S, when I could get a word in edgewise: So what do you do about a cavernous malformation? And what caused it? And will it do this again? And what made it do this in the first place???

Dr. S: Do? Well...nothing. I mean, if it were a (he didn't exactly say, but by now I had determined: "dreaded") AVM we would either surgically remove it (Me, to myself: how do you REMOVE a CAVERN???) or we close it off. With a cavernous malformation we first advise you not to use blood thinners, such as aspirin or Coumadin.

(Me, to myself: Great! So the fact that I was advised to take an aspirin a day following my "TIA" was grossly bad advice?) To Dr. S: So do you think taking the aspirin brought on the CCM bleed?

Dr. S: No, aspirin doesn't thin the blood that much.

(Me to myself: but you just said...I'm confused!)

Dr. S again: And we just monitor it, maybe do another MRI in a while to see what it's doing.

Me: So, what are the chances this could happen again?

He: Oh, not really much of a chance. (Me, to myself: that's NOT REALLY MUCH OF AN ANSWER!) I mean, they usually, pretty much, most of the time, don't bleed again. (Me, to myself: Wow! that's a crowd-pleaser! "Usually, pretty much"??? What you're saying is "it's a crap-shoot"!)

He: Well, I hope I haven't been throwing a lot of stuff at you that's confusing!

Me, meekly: No, it's fine. Thanks for calling. (really. I think...) so...what's next?

May Day

He: Well, I'm going to talk again to the radiologists and ask about the bleeding and the fact that we didn't see the CCM in 2006 and whether we should, in fact, do the angiogram to rule out an AVM (Me, to myself: in other words, you're still stumped! I'm still a neurological anomaly!) and I'll get back to you. But overall, this is good news.

Me, to myself: Really? How can that be? Now we just sort of have a name for the white thing (or not!) but no clear answer as to what to do next and how to prevent it from striking again! Although, I do feel a bit justified in knowing that it wasn't something I did that necessarily caused this. I mean, it wasn't high blood pressure or cholesterol. But still...

Later, at the computer...depending on who you believe (Mayo Clinic, Harvard Medical School, Wikipedia, WebMD, Department of Radiology and Nuclear Medicine of the Uniformed Services University of the Health Sciences, etc.) a cavernous malformation either looks like a mulberry or a raspberry! (so, no, it's not actually a "cavern" aka "hole" but why do they call it a "cavernous" malformation then? that doesn't make sense! why don't they call it a "fruity" malformation??), can cause seizures and/or brain bleeds or be asymptomatic (oh yeah, Dr. S. did mention seizures and headaches), be benign or KILL you! (Yeah, remember Flo Jo? Florence Johnson, flamboyant and famous Olympic runner? Did you know that she died at 38 of a seizure caused by a CAVERNOUS MALFORMATION???!!! Could have gone all night without reading that!), call for surgery or not...the more I investigated the more questions I had for Dr. S. He did say several times, "you have my card (actually I don't!), you can call me." But I'm not sure he wants to be barraged with all the questions I have floating in my head along with a berry.

This seems to be the way things are. Always more questions than answers...The biggest one to me now is: What now?

Anna Marie Porter

The Search for the Cure

Walk, Don't Run

Sep 3, 2011 1:02pm

Remember how in an earlier post I expressed a hope that I would be walking before Jack & Sophie? Well, I guess you could say that I have sort of achieved that albeit with help (AFO's, walkers, canes, railings, etc.) but I have been managing to get around much more so than even a month ago. And Jack & Sophie? Well, thankfully they are still behind me. But the thing is that they are doing this for the first time and, I'm pretty sure, are not having to "think" about it or remember what it was like before. Yes, I'm getting around but I'm not as fast as I once was and I can't maneuver stairs or slopes or uneven surfaces with the same assurance that I won't fall on my butt or my head! More therapy is definitely in order.

So I FINALLY got through the medical maze to resume PT. I had one session on August 15 and two last week. Can I just say, as an aside, that PT's as a group are annoyingly cheerful, energetic and positive-thinking?! A bunch of "Pollyanna's" as my mother would have said. I mean, I really appreciate that they are basically fun to be with but what do they have to be so gall-darned happy about?! Really?! Oh, yeah...they aren't the ones wearing AFO's and hobbling around with walkers and hoping against hope that they will walk before a couple of 1-year-olds!

At any rate, they are really a great bunch and fun to work with. And in outpatient PT they can try stuff we couldn't do at home. Like electro-shock therapy. That's right! Electric shock! Okay, maybe not exactly what we think of as EST but last week my PT Mary attached two very small electrical wires to my peroneus longus. Don't I sound smart?! Okay, for those of you who never passed biology, herewith is Wikipedia's definition: "In human anatomy, the peroneus longus (al-

so known as fibularis longus) is a superficial muscle in the lateral compartment of the leg, and acts to evert and plantar flex the ankle. It is situated at the upper part of the lateral side of the leg, and is the most superficial of the three peroneus muscles." Now do you know which one I'm talking about? Of course you don't! I mean, where the heck is the "lateral compartment of the leg," and what the heck does "evert" and "plantar flex" mean (they weren't even in my MS dictionary! Heck, it didn't even have peroneus!)?? And, by the way, I take offense – or perhaps my peroneus longus should – at the accusation that it is "superficial"! I can tell you there's nothing phony or shallow about it! (See MS thesaurus).

Okay. Forget the Latin/medical mumbo-jumbo. The muscle I'm referring to is the big one that lays along the outside of your calf and it is the one that helps counter-balance the muscles on the inner side of your calf that together can keep your foot straight when you take a step. Mine just happens to be lazy – or perhaps still sleeping after 3 months – and so the inner muscle is doing all the pulling. Hence my foot can only curl inward and a step with my right foot looks pretty danged strange. Here's another way to think of it: imagine being in a row boat out on a lake and laying the right oar down in the boat and only rowing with the left one. Got the image now?

Anyhoo...Mary attached two little wires to my...peroneus longus, and those wires were attached to a little transmitter which she could set to a reasonable level of electrical current to come and go in intervals. Every time the current would gradually increase on my muscle it would magically pull the foot into the proper position for a right-footed step. Once the current slacked off the muscle would too and my foot curled back in. It was cool to watch and amazing to think that this is precisely what our nerves and muscles are doing on a regular basis thousands of times and in hundreds of combinations every minute of every day! Did it hurt? Not a bit! It was a little weird at first but I have to say once I got used to it it actually felt kind of pleasant.

Kind of like sitting in a vibrating chair. And it worked so well that I wanted to take it home it me!

That's the most fun we have had in PT so far. The other big news is that I'm now into subtraction. That's right: science AND math! What I am subtracting is DME. (Remember your acronyms from about 2 months ago? DME is durable medical equipment.) I rarely use the wheelchair any more, not even as a desk chair. It is now sitting in the garage, intended only for use if I have really long distances to traverse. I also graduated from the walker to a quad cane. A quad cane is a cane with four small feet at the bottom instead of one. Making this "leap" reminds me of when Kyle had (accidentally!) totaled my Toyota Siena mini-van and when I went to the Toyota dealer to start car shopping again I told the salesman that I was ready to graduate from my soccer-mom minivan to something else. That's when I got my first SUV: a little sleeker, a little more grown-up. That's my cane. Not so in-your-face-I'm-old-before-my-time as the walker! I'm also "cheating" and not using the AFO (remember? Ankle-foot Orthotic?) around the house much at all and sometimes not even to walk to the nearest neighbors. In fact, I've taken to wearing a pair of sling-back flat flip flops or "walking" barefoot around the house. And those of you who have seen me have exclaimed at how well I'm getting around now!

But, I must confess. Mary basically pointed out that I've been "cheating." I mean, she didn't say it in so many words but I got her gist. In order to get around as fast as I possibly can I continue to put a lot of pressure on the left side, letting the right side slack off. The result? Some lower back pain on the left and a continued lazy right peroneus longus. When I'm really doing the work right, I have to actually slow down (!), put weight over on the right side (remember Weight Bear? He's still there prodding me!), try to bend the ankle forward and follow through with the right toes. How's that going you ask?

May Day

Have you ever asked someone a question that you know they might be reluctant to answer truthfully but you make it very clear that you want them to be honest no matter how disappointing the answer might be? And when you get that honest answer from them, the one that you sort of already had an inkling was the answer, and you sort of wish you hadn't asked the question and pressed for an honest answer? Well, I asked Mary the question: "Is it possible that I'll never regain feeling/function in the toes and/or foot on my right side?" This time Mary did not take the characteristic PT Pollyanna attitude. She answered honestly. Essentially what she said was that it was possible that there was actual damage (not just interruption of use) to the nerves there and in that case, perhaps not. Of course, then she went on to say how lucky I was to have gotten my hand/arm back because those are usually tougher to get back and that she was working with a patient who had been a musician and he lost the use of his hand and can't play an instrument any more.

But I didn't want to hear about how lucky I am! I didn't want to hear the "it-could-always-be-worse" story. I know. The stroke could have killed me. I could have lost eyesight, hearing, and cognitive ability; swallowing or talking...I know all that! I am SO lucky! But this is MY experience, from MY vantage point. And I want to walk...and yes, RUN, again and be able to move quickly to rescue a grandchild who might be about to do something dangerous and stroll on the beach with my husband and dog, and stand up on tiptoe to reach that glass pitcher or platter, and climb a ladder and get into my sloping garden and...There is more to life than just the ability to type and prepare food and wash your own hair. I know that I am lucky that I have what I have...I want MORE!

Lest you all worry, I am not giving up or giving in. I will continue to go to PT two times a week. I will continue to work on wiggling my toes and helping my brain make that connection. I will continue to do my leg/foot exercises at home...when the pain in my gut doesn't interfere. Oh that? That's a story for another time...

Anna Marie Porter

Two For the Price of One

Sep 27, 2011 11:25am

So, you thought this blog was all about a single medical event. You didn't know you were going to get more than your money's worth, did you!

Sometimes it takes a little time and perseverance to figure out medical mysteries. Just ask Dr. House's crack team! Remember my little trip to the ER in early July? We thought I was having the heart attack follow-up to my stroke? Well, we know it wasn't a heart attack and now we know it wasn't food poisoning or GERD or some virus either. After I had a couple more minor episodes I took myself straight to my gastroenterologist. (Yes, I have a gastroenterologist. I've had a few tummy problems, so what?). Anyway, he said all this sounded like my gall bladder! So, off to another set of ultrasounds (cuz I also mentioned the ongoing pain in my lower abdomen). The next day I got a call from his office. They got the results of the ultrasound. Everything looked normal. Great! My innards are "normal" and I'm CRAZY! Fine...so my gut just likes to attack me every now and then. I get it.

A few hours later the GI Dr.'s office called again. They didn't realize there were two ultrasounds done. The results of the second one just came in. "You have sludge in your gall bladder." "Sludge?" "Yes, you have sludge in your gall bladder." "What is 'sludge'?" "Well, it's when you have pulverized gall stones mixed with mucus. (mmmmm...sounds lovely!) It's really worse than gall stones because it can plug up the valves easier (I'm feeling more like an old jalopy all the time). But the doctor wants you to do a blood test to be sure that's what's causing the pain. I'll send you the lab order. Then next time you're having symptoms go to the nearest lab and have them do the test." "You mean, whenever I'm having the pains again, just go to a lab? What if it's the ["frikkin"] middle of the night?" "Then you can just go the nearest emergency room. They can order the lab work there. Oh, and you might want to avoid any fatty foods until you get the lab paperwork, just in case."

Are you kidding me? Okay, first of all, I'd like to say in my defense that I didn't intentionally pulverize my gall stones. It's just sorta happened! And let's talk frankly about "sludge." Sludge? That's the best the medical community can do? They can come up with "diaphoresis" for "sweat" but all they can think of for what is the equivalent of "wastewater" in my gall bladder is "sludge"??? Really? And now they want me to hie myself to the nearest lab, day or night when I'm solely dependent on everyone else to drive me to get some blood drawn? Really? That's the "scientific" way to test this theory out?

And what causes sludge to form in the gall bladder anyway? Well, first of all, the GI Dr (you know, and why is it "GI" Dr? Shouldn't it be "GE" Dr? Isn't he a doctor of gastro-ENterology? It's not "gastro-INterology." Why is it GI Dr.?? GI stands for "gastro-intestinal." Why isn't he a doctor of "gastro-intestinalogy"? Why, if the plural of goose is geese, isn't the plural of moose "meese"?...) told me at my office visit that women in their 40's & 50's are more prone to gall bladder issues. And why is that?? Aren't women in their 40's & 50's suffering enough from pre-, menopause, and post-? It figures.

So a quick visit to our favorite medical library (aka Google search) reveals that the following can cause "sludge" to form in the gall bladder:

1. *Being a woman (okay, that one fits)*
2. *Being Native American (nope)*
3. *Diabetes (nope. not yet anyway.)*
4. *Rapid weight loss or starvation diets (not a chance!)*
5. *Organ transplant (not me either)*

So, what you're telling me is that I am simply blessed with this decidedly un-classy-sounding muck in my gall bladder by virtue of the fact that I have x chromo-somes??? And what, pray tell, do they do about sludge? My Operations Manager wonders if they can't just "vacuum" it out somehow?! To listen to my pal, Dr. Tom, I should have them rip the sucker out! No sense in bothering with it. It's not an essential organ anyway.

So, let's talk about that. What is the gall bladder, why is it there and why can we live without it just as easily as with it? The way I understand it, the gall bladder is sorta like a turkey baster. It takes in bile (which the liver invents) and stores it there and then, conveniently squirts that bile out into the intestines when food comes down the pike.

So, it's definitely the sludge causing the pain. Two weeks later I have a minor attack (thankfully during regular office hours) and we go to the local walk-in clinic. A blood test done and results sent to the GI Dr. office and a phone call later confirms this. Well, thank God. I really WASN'T making this up! Back into the doctor office, this time to see the GI Dr.'s partner who says I basically have 3 choices (which really don't seem like balanced choices at all):

1. *Do nothing (which he doesn't recommend. Really? That's a choice??);*

2. *Do surgery (remember, the gall bladder isn't really necessary. Surgery is a CHOICE? We CHOOSE to have surgery? Who in his/her right mind would CHOOSE to have surgery unless it's to smooth out some wrinkles or make a nose smaller?);*

3. *Try some medication which is designed to dissolve sludge (you mean like the chemicals they use for an oil spill?).*

"Anna Porter...you choose! Door #1, Door #2 or Door #3!"

May Day

Well, we know #1 is not really an option now that, well, we KNOW. #2 seems extreme if there's a chance of keeping the GB. I mean, it supposedly isn't really necessary but I've heard some not-so-appealing first-hand reviews. #3 seems the logical choice. Right Dr? I mean, clearly you were steering me in that direction anyway. I know how this "psychology" thing works! Okay, write the prescription. "We'll do another ultrasound in 3 months to see if it's working."

That was Thursday. Didn't pick up the Rx until Friday. Saturday a.m., about 2:00 woke up to the second worst pain in my gut (the first being the one we thought was a heart attack). Tried to fight it off with gas meds, heat, different positions, even Benadryl© to just put me to sleep to forget it. No deal. By 7:00 I was crying "uncle." Called the GI Dr. office to see if there was a doctor on call. She called back a couple of excruciating minutes later. I explained everything in a nutshell and asked if there was anything I could do for the pain. "There's nothing you can do. You need to get the closest ER and have them remove it."

What?? Just like that? March into Providence Everett ER and announce that they are to remove my gall bladder??? Okay. If you say so.

David dutifully drives me to the ER, AGAIN! "Name?" "Anna Porter." "Birth date?" "3-31-58." "Oh, yes, here you are." At this point David tried to interject some humor. "Yes, my wife is collecting frequent-flier miles!" (Funny. Just either give me something for the pain or shoot me!)

Finally laying down in my ER bed the doctor mercifully has the nurse inject me with some morphine. Pain? Gone! What did that doc-on-call mean, there's nothing that can be done for the pain! I feel great now! Another ultrasound. This technician feels it necessary to give me a biology lesson at the same time. "So, this is your stomach. And this is your aorta, the large artery that supplies blood to your intestines. And this is your..." Look, I think but don't say. It all looks like a bunch of gray and white blobs to me. You could be pointing at my kidney and calling it my lung for all I know. Would you just get on with it? I don't want to seem mean but I really just don't care at this point and besides, trying to look at the screen for your little demonstration is giving me a crick in my neck!

"Well, I don't see any sludge in your gall bladder." He pronounces it as if he has just declared that Long Island is, in fact, not an island. Oh, good. Either the GI doctors and the last radiologist and the lab techs are complete morons or the pain is being caused by my gall bladder instantaneously ejecting all the sludge as we gaze on! What do you mean there isn't any sludge in my gall bladder! The GALL!! I was counting on knowing what was causing this horrible pain! Now what???

"But I do see sand. And that's worse.(what? worse than sludge, which is worse that stones???) But I'll have the radiologist look these over and the dr. will get back to you."

*What?! Sand? Are you kidding me? Are you people just making this sh*t up or what??? And why did you see SAND when the other radiologist saw SLUDGE? And what do you mean sand is worse? It certainly sounds better than sludge. Yeah. Better to have a beach in your gall bladder than an oil slick!*

Dr. ER returns to confirm that yes, I have sand but

surgery is really elective at this point. (Wait, elective? You mean like COSMETIC? You mean like having my teeth straightened-or-doing-a- tummy-tuck-elective? So I can ELECT to have pain or NOT?!) They sent me home with some anti-nausea meds, some pain meds and the name of a surgeon. So much for marching into ER and demanding gall bladder removal.

May Day

I call my GI Dr's assistant on Monday and tell her my sob story. She relays it to the Dr. He responds, through her, that I can either try the meds for a while or arrange for surgery. You mean, like I just call up any ol' surgeon and arrange my own surgery? This really is starting to sound like cosmetic surgery! Doesn't the GI Dr. usually refer patients? Well, he could give me some names or I could call a surgeon closer to me. My choice. Doesn't sound like much of a choice...Meantime, I'll just be taking my pills (which, according to the Google Medical Library have a snowball's chance in hell of dissolving the sludge/sand and if it does it could take months...OR YEARS!!!) and just to tempt fate I'm loading up on the fatty foods!!

In It for the Long Haul

Oct 20, 2011 8:24pm

My PT is a Nazi! No, not in the literal sense, but she does seem to have a bit of SS Officer in her! I mean, she's nice enough. At least she pretends to be. But they all do. On the outside they are always smiling and cheerful--you know, Pollyanna-ish--all the while scheming new ways to inflict torture. She even admitted as much to me today. Said she is always planning new ways to torture me! Do you need more proof??

Four weeks ago she added to my regular at-home regimen. She had me lay on my side, and told me to lift my leg at the hip, out toward the back THIRTY times! Then she smiled sadistically and said, "That's right, I said THIRTY!" The only thing she refrained from doing was chuckling cruelly out loud! Then she told me to do the same on the other side. Then, when I was already nearly fainting from exhaustion she put a big PT wedge pillow under the top leg and told me to raise the lower leg another THIRTY times on EACH SIDE!! Are you getting the complete picture here? But wait, there's more! Then she had me lay on my stomach, tied a 2-lb weight to my bad ankle and instructed me to bend my knee and raise the foot up 10 times! Finally, before I left she assigned me to continue doing these exercises at home, but to increase the side lifts to 50-100 times each (in her notes to me she said, "Yes, I typed that correctly.") and the foot raises (starting without the weight--how generous!) 50 times and when I could do 50 times "smoothly" to add the 1-2# weight, start out at 10 times and work my way back up to 50 AND to keep going until I can do 10 to 15 POUNDS!!! And those were only 2 of the exercises she gave me that day. She printed them all out neatly on a form that's entitled (is it "entitled" or "titled"? I'm never quite sure!): "Personal Exercise Program" like it's from some exclusive health club or something.

"How is physical therapy going?" people frequently ask. Well, I'm making progress, I guess. Let me try to help you grasp what that "progress" is like. Imagine that you are loading a large dump truck with sand, by yourself. Imagine that you are doing this with a teaspoon. Now imagine that in addition, you are blindfolded. Get the picture? Yes, yes, yes...I'm MAKING PROGRESS! (I was reminded the other day of something someone who was a client at the low-income service provider I worked for said years ago: "I would hate to die with so much potential.") Yes, if you had been one of the "lucky ones" to visit me in the hospital and had not seen me since you would be "amazed" by "how far" I've come! You would gasp excitedly, remembering how when you saw me last I could barely raise my arm by myself and was ambulating in a wheelchair. Yes, you would say how "lucky" I am to have the full use of my hand and arm back (yes, I know "how many people never get that back."). You would note with glee how I'm "WALKING" by myself with the use of only a quad cane and sometimes without any extra device. You would remind me that it has all happened so quickly too! And you would remark that I'm young and strong and determined and that you are just sure I'll make a full recovery.

I had a stroke nearly 5 months ago. I've never seen a "stroke recovery calendar" so it's hard to know what is quick or not. How long should it take to gain back the use of one's extremities after a stroke? At what point do people stop noting how quickly you are healing and start saying, "well, this is about how far you should expect to be after ________ months/years."? Is it kind of like the "Baby's Age Reference Calendar"? You know, how for a while it's how many hours old, then it's how many days old, then it's weeks, then it's years and years-and-a-half." Then there is this magic moment (it's never really quite clear when but it must be written down somewhere in a parent's guide because we all know it) when we just refer to the age of our offspring in full years. The stroke recovery calendar must be like that. And I can't help but wonder: at what point have you reached the limits of that calendar and where you are is where you are. Of course, when I ponder this aloud--or in writing--my friends and family immediately rush to my aide with words of encouragement. "Don't give up! You'll get there! You're young and strong! It just will take time! You just have to be patient!"

I just think it would have been handy if there had been some warranty with the process. You know, some reference guide that would let you know about where you should expect to be by a certain time based on your age, the severity of the stroke, the impact, etc. This "nobody-knows-for-sure-everyone-is-so-different" assessment just isn't cutting it! So, then, what do people in my situation do? We look to the experience of others. We listen for stories of people who's calamity somewhat matches ours (i.e. fits an imaginary checklist of similarities that we just make up) and find out what their recovery rate is/was. That's why, the other day I was pleased to hear from Mattie that she had spoken with our insurance agent and when she mentioned what had happened to me our agent shared that her mother had also had a stroke (check one) that partially paralyzed her (check two)and that her leg/foot were the last things to come back (check three) but she did get them back finally after two years. Wait...what??!! TWO YEARS??!! Crap! But there were enough similarities that I decided to get it straight from "the horse's mouth" and asked our agent myself. Yes, she confirmed all of that but pointed out that her mother had been in her late 70's (okay, well maybe I have a "leg up" on her...pardon the pun!). But she had to ruin it all by adding "but she was in really good shape." Well, that cinches it! What I gained by my younger age she eclipsed by "being in really good shape"!

I had no idea how bad of shape I am in. Back in PT she is working on things like strengthening leg, hip, and butt muscles. She's having me do balancing practice. She's encouraging many repetitions. She's exhausting me! I have to honestly say that I'm not sure how much of this stuff I could have done before the stroke! And now I am working with muscles that are not quite connecting with the brain. In fact, these muscles have clearly FORGOTTEN they had ever been used before! What are my chances now?? You probably don't remember this but learning how to walk, to get all of the muscles, ligaments, joints, tendons, nerves necessary to work together to simply bend your knee, lift your foot, bending at the ankle and then the toes, clearing the floor then planting it down a foot or so ahead, heel first, then arch then toes all organized by the "mission control room" that is your brain--doing all of that to just take a step forward IS EXHAUSTING when you actually have to think about it and focus on it and do it! No wonder toddlers need two naps a day and get cranky a lot! Today I was getting exhausted from just kneeling on the exercise mat and "walking" on my knees while pushing a foam wedge for support for just 6 "steps"! This is clearly going to take more effort than I thought...and clearly more work than the brochure led me to believe!

So you might have noticed by my "quick update" that I have officially moved back upstairs to our bedroom. Yes, I did it. It just seemed like I might as well, even though I am not allowed to carry ANYTHING as I traverse up and down the stairs and my husband is NOT HAPPY that sometimes I go up and down by myself! And even though going up and down is a process that takes a good 3 minutes or more and careful attention to each step along the way. And even though I still have to go downstairs to shower where there are handrails. And even though I have a little trouble getting into and out of bed as it is a tad higher off the floor than my little twin bed was. Yes, even so, we have done the move and the office is now back to being an office. Progress...I guess...

The New Math

Dec 4, 2011 9:46am

I can't shake the idea that having a stroke is a mathematical equation. I subtracted a whole lot on May 23, have added and subtracted much in between, and while the equations get smaller, continue with simple math (luckily there has been little multiplying!)

Since I last wrote I subtracted the wheelchair. I am able to walk even long distances (albeit slowly) without the help of wheels. I have subtracted not only the walker but also my "quad cane" (a cane with four "feet" instead of one). I have therefore added a single pole cane. This is no ordinary cane. Kyle assisted me in choosing a stylish faux wood burl cane that breaks down like a tent pole (yes, I do feel like a British spy when I whip it out and it snaps into place!). I mean, if you have to walk with a cane it might as well draw attention!

And speaking of long distances, I have added nearly daily walking my dog again. Actually, sometimes it amounts to him dragging me a bit (even more than before as I'm more unsteady on my feet) but we are making it even uphill a little. Of course, coming back down hill is a bit unnerving at times but I haven't fallen, yet!

Unfortunately by using the single pole cane I have added "tennis elbow." No, I did not get it by playing tennis or even by practicing my swing with the cane! And I resent the fact that this fairly common malady among many folks who don't play tennis – and perhaps have never even raised a racquet – bears a name that only makes the afflicted feel worse for having not received the injury from a sporting event!

In any event, you can get "tennis elbow" from walking with a cane and putting too much faith in, er pressure on it. No one had the common courtesy to tell me this before I started using it and now I'm paying the price. I have also added a stylish armband designed to apply the necessary pressure to the inflamed tendon below the sore secsection to alleviate strain. I have also added a handy neoprene wrap that keeps an ice pack in place on the elbow. And I have subtracted activities that make it hurt more. So far, I am resisting the suggestion by my physiatrist and my PT to add OT as a method to heal it.

I have also subtracted some procedures and the accompanying doctor's visits. I will NOT be having brain surgery. The head doctors all agree now that my stroke was caused by a cavernous malformation (no, not a big hole in my brain but a cluster of blood vessels that hang out on the brain tissue and decide for no apparent reason to hemorrhage or cause seizures) and they don't operate on those (especially where mine is located). What do they do? "Keep an eye on them" which is to say, "Wait and see if they cause any more problems." But well, no more visits to head doctors.

I have also subtracted heart surgery. Since it has finally been determined that my stroke was NOT caused by my PFO (patent foramen ovale, aka hole between the ventricles) I do not have to have it closed up. Also, minus the incumbent doctor appointments. (And by way, I am inclined to digress momentarily from the topic to mention that both the cavernous malformation and the PFO are items one is born with. What the heck? Did I not go through a quality-control check before entering this world??)

I have, so far, subtracted gall bladder surgery as well. My GI doc prescribed a medication that in his words "might work but may take time" to dissolve either the sludge or the sand (depending on who's reading the ultrasounds) that was causing blockage and pain. I am happy to say – whether it's really a miracle drug or just the placebo effect – that I have been gall-bladder-pain free since my last visit to

ER! Therefore I have also subtracted the ER visits and those doctor visits!

On the plus side (gee, that was pun-y!) I have added pounds which is to say I am more of a plus side. Well, that's just not fair! So now that I'm back to getting more physical exercise I have GAINED weight? Maybe it's muscle?? Or maybe it's because I've also added cooking the family meals back into my daily regimen? This a plus that I'm pleased with. Cooking is therapy for me; I actually do it for fun!

What I'd really like to add now is a working foot, knee, hip and leg. Sigh...

Graduation Day

Dec 12, 2011 4:35pm

Last Thursday, December 8 was graduation day for me. I have "graduated" from formal PT and am now on my own. It has been a long time since I graduated from college but I am reminded that it was pretty much the same thing: the "system" determines that it has filled your brain full of as much information as it can impart and so now you are supposed to go forth into the world and make something of that information. I'm feeling much as I did then: "What am I supposed to do now?!"

This is not how I pictured it. In my mind, graduation from PT was going to take place when I had regained my ability to walk and that was going to happen maybe by the end of September or October at the outside. I never imagined that one day I'd be discharged and told good luck, just keep practicing what you've learned here and someday maybe you'll be as good as new! So now, it's up to me...this is nothing like I had "planned."

This means that I am supposed to keep exercising EVERY day. Did I ever mention that I really don't LIKE to exercise? It just isn't my cup of tea. I mean, I like walking and some bike riding (on flat surfaces!) and I'll swim on occasion but actual exercise...like doing leg lifts, etc...yuck! And now it's up to me to make sure I'm doing them? when I don't see HUGE improvement as a result? I mean, I'm still not WALKING!

I know, those of you who have seen me would disagree. You would say you've seen me "walking." But what I really do is "get around." My Ops. Manager, Kelly says that she and I are the "queens of the 'work around.'" If something doesn't work the way it is "supposed" to we figure out another way. That's what I do to get from point A to point B. I have learned a "work around" to "get around" but it's not officially "walking."

Walking is a whole other thing that we learn and by gum it appears that I have completely forgotten how! Or at least my right side has forgotten! So now I am having to learn all over again but this time it's not "natural" learning; my head is filled with all kinds of nuances that I'm supposed to remember: lift knee, bend foot at ankle, bend foot at toes, lift off, set heel down first with ball of foot facing outward, roll down to big toe then other toes, and don't scrunch down in the abdomen and stand up straight, don't lean too much to the left, balance your weight, and...! Remember learning to drive a standard shift car? I thought I would never figure it out! But that was nothing like learning to walk again. If you don't believe me, just slow down for a moment and observe every little movement each part of your body makes just so you can move forward. See what I mean??? Not so easy is it?

Part of the problem is memory. No, not my memory! My muscle memory. Turns out muscles have them too--and can lose them! So, for instance, after I have slept for a while my leg turns into a limp, dead weight because the muscles FORGOT to keep working. Really?? They FORGOT??!! So I have to keep reminding them to work. Which means I have to REMEMBER to REMIND them!! What a ridiculous predicament. We (my muscles & I) are like a couple of Alzheimer patients trying to take care of each other! This should be interesting...

I guess this is as good a time as any to graduate from this blog as well. From here on out the postings could get pretty dull unless I make stuff up! But here's the deal: those of you who keep bugging me to turn this experience into a book, here's your chance to help make it happen! These days, publishers are more interested in authors who have a following already. And one way they measure that is through the traffic at the writer's blog. So, here is what you do...go right now to: iamawriterinmymind.blogspot.com and click on "Follow this Blog." Also, you can sign up for email reminders and/or an RSS feed (if you know how these work let me know!) so you can keep up with my blog. But the most important thing is to get the number of followers up! So please do this and then INVITE FRIENDS to follow! I don't care if they know me or not, or if they want to read the blog! I just need followers and I will beg, borrow or steal them!

Thank you all for the love, prayers, thoughts, well-wishes, laughs and support. You are all a godsend to me; I cannot tell you what having you there has meant for my recovery! Please do keep in touch and do check out my continuing saga via my writer's blog! Love to you all!

It really is like graduation. It's as if they're saying, "We've stuffed your brain full of things, we've helped you practice them along the way, but now you have to take what you've learned and go out into the world and do something with it—whatever you decide to do."

So that's that...*or is it?*

Anna Marie Porter

While Waiting for the New PT to Begin

Vocal Note: Can I just say?...I hate this…I hate one more time explaining to a medical care provider what happened & why. I hate even having to go through this. I feel like it's a waste of time…

Back in therapy. No, not that kind! Although I probably need that more. No, my primary care doc wasn't satisfied that I wasn't driving or riding a bike or running marathons! She decided I should go back into physical therapy to see if strength training would help. She wants to "see [me] riding around the neighborhood on my grown-up tricycle." Wow. That's not something I'd wanna see! One step closer to old lady-hood. First the chronic sports shoe attire, then the fanny pack (which I now refuse to wear!), then the tricycle, then…Oh no! Not the appliquéd sweatshirt! Aaagggghhhhh!

I want my goals to include being able to wear at least a kitten heel again! Maybe be able to climb up on a stool to reach the cookie cutters in the upper cupboards. Or how about being able to get down on the floor (and back up again) to play with my grandchildren (instead of feeling like they're my great-grandchildren and I'm some frail octogenarian). Riding a tricycle at the age of 54 is definitely not on my bucket list.

So, back to PT I go. I try another facility—this one sportier since my doc wants me to use "more machines." (Frankly I prefer kitchen machines but they don't improve my legs). At my first appointment there is the obligatory "story-of-my-life" and why I'm in therapy and what I want to accomplish (as though I have some say in what that will be). We talk about the dreaded tone and the therapist asks me again when this happened and how much I've improved in the last few months (not much). He: "Well, if the tone hasn't improved much more by now it probably won't." Then he runs me through some exercises and walking to see what my condition is. I'm rather taken aback when he announces, "Wow. That's some pretty significant tone! I see why you're not driving! I'm personally glad you're not!" (Me, to myself,: "Well, thanks a lot! That makes me feel great!")

So, we focus on strength and balance. Turns out I'm not bad in either department. I think he was surprised. He sends me home with some exercises (Great. More exercises. I love exercising.). And we part.

Today, my third visit, I get up the nerve (I don't know why that's so hard! I mean, it's my body and my time and my recovery but I just have trouble asking the tough questions) to ask: "So, you said at my first visit that if the tone hasn't improved more by now it probably won't. If that's the case, what is the treatment goal?" (to myself: "Aha! I gotcha! Now you have to 'fess up—you're just doing this to a) make more money for the clinic; or b) justify your existence; or c) satisfy my primary care doc's misguided notions about riding tricycles!")

He pauses. He knows he's been had! Then he says, "Well, we're gonna try to strengthen what you do have."

Hmmm...it's lame, but it's an answer. I don't feel all that weak but who knows. I guess I'll give it a try. I peddle faster on the stationary bike just to show off. See, I'm in pretty good shape! I even get myself off the bike with no assistance! So there! Then they try to challenge me with tougher routines and trickier moves but I meet the challenge and he is pleasantly surprised. And...so am I.

So when do you say "when"? Just when I'm prepared to throw in the towel and concede that this is the best it's going to get I make a tiny, scarcely-noticeable-but-undeniable-hair's-width improvement. But, you say, that's good, isn't it? Isn't that encouraging?

It is encouraging but it is also unsettling. How does one manage in a world of "maybe…maybe…maybe…no!...but maybe…maybe…maybe…yes!...maybe…maybe…maybe…no!...but …

I am reminded of a trip to emergency years ago with my elderly, infirm aunt. I cannot remember the exact circumstances of why but I do remember that for some reason the emergency room staff decided that it was imperative that they get a "blood gasses" test. If you have never had—or seen—this done consider yourself lucky (or warned!). It is one of the most excruciating blood tests I can imagine. It requires tapping into an artery, rather than the more benign veins, because it is used to measure the level of oxygen in the oxygen-rich blood. What this means to the patient is that the phlebotomist has to hit an artery and those tend to lie farther below the surface and aren't seen but rather "felt" by the needle. It sometimes requires an initial puncture and then a rooting around with the needle subcutaneously until an artery is struck. (Yeah! I told you!)

Back in the army hospital ER with my aunt there was a bit of hand-wringing (and perhaps "straw- drawing") about deciding who would be the lucky…er, most qualified person to do the blood draw. In the end, one of the more senior nurses was elected and she came in to do the prep. While she was prepping, my aunt (who had been the unfortunate "victim" of previous blood gas draws) was prepping herself mentally, physically and emotionally for this very painful procedure (and not very well, at that). Her method of prep was to grip whatever was close to her hands, including one of mine; tightening every other muscle in her body; grimacing; and moaning a little. The nurse swabbed my aunt's arm, raised her needle, took aim, sucked in her breath and then...suddenly got called away to a greater emergency! I thought my aunt was going to faint or stop breathing! She collapsed like a balloon that is filled with air and then let go to sputter and zoom until it deflates and falls to the ground.

Three times (yes, three!) the nurse went through the same drill and three times she got called away! When she finally plunged in the needle the tension in the room was palpable. And then she began to "dig" for the artery and I thought my aunt was going to stand upright from her prone position. Even I started feeling nauseous and faint. And then, the nurse stopped mining and removed the needle. She had been unsuccessful.

She left the room and returned with one of the EMT's who had only seen the procedure done but was willing to give it a try. By now my aunt was ready to just give up on being healed. Luckily he was successful on the first attempt but frankly I'm surprised he found any blood to test as I would have expected it to have drained from my poor aunt's body by then.

Why tell this gruesome tale? The starts and stops of the needle test are a metaphor for the hope and despair of uncertain recovery. You walk to the precipice not knowing if you'll achieve flight or sink like a stone. And after a while you just can't take the stress of the unknown so it's easier to stay away from the cliff altogether.

Twice in three sessions my PT has firmly stated that if I had not overcome the tone by 10 months' time that I would not overcome it. I was ready to declare in the words of Alexander Pope, "Whatever is, is right." But at the end of today's session there was a look in my PT's eyes that said, "Okay. Maybe I was wrong. Maybe, just maybe..."

It's Not Walking. Walking is a Whole Other Thing.

I've probably said this before (and most likely will say it again) but if one more person says "Look at you! You're walking!" I'm gonna scream! This, this thing that I do to ambulate from one place to another, this is *not* walking! Not in any sense of the word. This is *getting around.* Walking is a whole *other* thing.

Walking, in case you were unaware, is a complex exercise in which brain, muscle, tendon, nerve, bone, cartilage, and blood dance together, perfectly choreographed. Human walking is frequently described as "controlled falling." According to the American Physiology Society..."walking does not involve a simple sequence of alternating contractions in pairs of antagonistic muscles but involves complex and variable patterns of activity."

Still not convinced? Take a few steps and carefully observe. As you move forward you bend your knee slightly, pull up your foot starting with the heel rolling up to your toes and then using your hip you'll propel yourself forward, generally with a great deal of grace and balance. Take any of those myriad muscles, joints, etc. out of the equation and regular walking—as we have evolved to do—no longer exists. It now becomes "getting around." In truth, I do *walk* with my left foot but I *manage* to drag my right foot along for the ride. When I try to gently bend my right foot forward (which it doesn't want to do) the action causes the right lower leg to jerk up marching style and the foot to curl inward resulting in putting the foot back down mostly on its side. If I try to force the natural movements of a step I end up dragging my toes along the floor and if I'm walking on carpet that's a recipe for tripping and/or stumbling.

I have a new appreciation for such a lowly activity as walking.[33] It is really poetry in motion compared to what I do. And walking is only part of it. I also can't kneel, can't squat down very well, have trouble rolling over in bed or on an exam table, crawling, and crouching under, and forget about getting down on the floor—at least on purpose! Not only are these activities nearly impossible but painful as well. So what, you say? Try picking something up that has fallen and rolled under a piece of furniture without squatting or kneeling.

Stepping over even a bump in the sidewalk or down from a curb can be treacherous. I do not have good leverage with my right leg so getting into and out of a restaurant booth or theater seat is tough. I lack the finesse to stand and just place my right foot into a shoe or even put on pants. I get tangled up in cords, table and chair legs, and other would-be obstacles. We can't park too close to another car as I can no longer squeeze out through a narrow passage, not being able to bend my knee sufficiently or slide my foot and let it out smoothly. There's definitely no scrambling up on a step stool or ladder to reach something above my head. And of course, driving—at least using my feet—is out of the question.

Perhaps the worst injustice: I am consigned to wearing only very flat, flexible, "sturdy" shoes, ones which are large enough

[33] Especially since we recently saw a robot on TV that can even walk up and down stairs…without a cane!

to accommodate my charming AFO. No heels, slip-ons, boots or skimpy sandals for me. And I have a pretty respectable collection of those! Every day I walk into my closet and am confronted by the Ferragamos, Eagles, Clarks, Italian Shoe Companies, and others that reside there. It is as if their collective eyes are gazing up at me; as if their collective voices are calling "remember"? They are decidedly from *before* and as time goes on and more than one expert tells me that this is probably the best it is going to get I wonder if it isn't the prudent thing to do to find a new home for them. But then I would walk into my closet and be confronted by sadly empty shoe shelves, looking as pathetic as when they were once filled with unused shoes.

At a birthday party I mentioned this in conversation with a friend. Her advice (because it seems that everyone has some for me these days!) was to start by giving up just my least favorite shoes and as I buy new ones that work I gradually give up the rest, eliminating the dreaded empty-shelf syndrome. Sound advice except...I'm also "paralyzed" by something similar to what families of coma victims must experience: when do you pull the plug? What if you pull it and then they come up with a cure? What if you pull it and then spend the rest of your life wondering if it was the right thing to do?[34]

Stigma

I like to pride myself in not being prejudiced. I think of myself as pretty open and accepting. But it's a delusion. Just like everyone, I can be discriminatory toward certain groups of people—and I hate myself for that. I particularly hate myself

---

[34] Also, with medical bills mounting, new shoes might be out of the question—leaving nothing but an empty, dusty set of shelves.

now that I am one who carries the...stigma. I cringe now when I think of how I have had disdain for others whom I perceive as having "made their own beds." Because now I could easily inspire similar thoughts by others.

Here I am...getting around with a limp and a cane and I wonder how many people who see me think, "Well of course she has trouble walking! She's obese!" Or when I tell people I had a stroke, "Well, that's no surprise, look how overweight she is! She probably has clogged arteries!" I can't help it. I have been known to have such thoughts and I can't be the only judgmental person who has had them. Even my own primary care physician, who clearly knows my history, keeps bringing up my high cholesterol when discussing my stroke. Sometimes I think she doesn't believe that it was caused by something else.

If my physical appearance doesn't trigger disdain it might also inspire pity. I don't know which is worse actually. Whatever the emotion, it makes me feel like I'm on parade, a sad addition to a sideshow. I hate being the center of attention—good or bad—but it's pretty hard to avoid when I'm gimping around.

I am learning a lot about myself, my opinions, and my responses to others. It is a hard lesson to learn.

Driving Miss Crazy

We make a lot of assumptions—and assume that we must find solutions—based on personal experience and cultural norms. For instance, we might assume that a single person is not single by choice so we'll encourage him by trying to play matchmaker. Or we might assume that a childless woman is just that because she *can't* have children, not because she *chooses not to*. Or that something must be done to get that reclusive widow back out into the world because, well, she just couldn't be happy being on her own all the time.

One of my favorite stories that demonstrates this tendency is when my second son was four. My mother had recently died—much too young—and our family had all attended her memorial service. Back at home a few weeks later I was working in the kitchen and Kyle was playing quietly alone not far away. Then suddenly he approached me. "Mama," he began his query, "Nana was your mama, right?" "Yes," I replied. "And Nana died." "Yes," again. I could almost "see" the wheels of his little brain working on this human algebraic equation. So next, logically, "So that means you don't have a mama." "No, not anymore."

The sheer emotional weight of that conclusion must have been sinking in as he remained silent for a while. Then, suddenly and brightly he bounced back. "I know!" he exclaimed, as though he had been called upon to find a solution. And he had. He had ticked off in his mind all the potential "mama" figures that were left to us: his GeeGee (his father's grandmother) and his Gramma (his father's mother) were still alive and available for the job. "GeeGee can be *daddy's* mama and Gramma can be *your* mama!" And with that he mentally rubbed his hands together as if to announce that the problem was solved, the problem that only a four-year-old could truly appreciate: *no one* should be without a mama.

I think this phenomenon is responsible for the numbers of people who feel the need to suggest solutions to my not driving. The assumption is that from their perspectives not being able to drive would be a fate worse than death and therefore I must have the same outlook. They also assume—presumably!—that

May Day

I'm not driving because I just hadn't thought about the solution that they are about to put forth.

Year ago I announced to a dear friend (a woman who is 10 years my senior and whose children were entering college when mine were just entering school) that I was pregnant with a little surprise—our fourth child. I was shocked by the intensity of her irate response and the venomous attack on the supposed irresponsibility of my husband! In a word, she was furious at him for doing *that* to me! Later she revealed the cause of her anger—she had responded not as she would as my friend but as if it were she who was again pregnant. Projecting herself into my situation, ten years older and thoroughly done with raising children, she naturally had severe anxiety which manifested itself in rage.

So it seems to be with my friends who would empathize with my predicament. Now I know you all mean well. And I know you might just find this hard to believe. But I just *don't miss driving*!! Really I don't! I'm not just saying that because I can't and I don't see any solution to the problem. I really don't mind it. I know! I'm surprised to hear it coming from my own lips but it appears to be true for me. It is rare that I feel trapped by not being able to hop into my car and drive anywhere I wish. I feel quite content to be driven where I need to go, perhaps in part because I don't feel a need to go too many places. I especially don't feel a need to go where your kind advice is driving me!

Recently I've begun to have dreams about driving—or contemplating driving—and then remembering that I can't.

Graduated from PT—*Again*

So, I wonder...is this like I now have my Masters in being a PT patient? When my eight week "prescription" was used up I was graduated from PT *again*. My physical therapist confirmed once again that "what I've got is what I've got" and there really wasn't anything more that they can do for me. This is not necessarily a happy graduation day. On the other hand, it might be nice to finally just *know* the truth—that I am as recovered from my stroke as I'm going to be and that's that and that's all. There's just no point in prolonging my date with reality. The sooner I come to grips with that the sooner I can just move on. But still...there's always *acupuncture!*[35]

Airplane Travel

It is so easy to forget (I know, I use the excuse frequently now that I had a stroke thus expunging myself for my lack of memory) that I have limitations with which I am unfamiliar. This is never so true as when I contemplated traveling by air for the first time. It used to be such a simple thing—decide to go somewhere, buy a ticket, pack a bag, and take off! But things are different now—boy *are* they! At a month out from my one-year anniversary I learned that my darling grandson was scheduled for a surgery we knew would one day come. He was born with *syndactily*, his own little "handicap," a condition in which two or more digits (usually fingers) remain fused together, remnants of the fetal flippers once comprised of five sets of bones covered together in mittens of flesh. In Jackie's case, the middle and ring fingers of his right hand were joined together as one with a single oversized fingernail and what appeared to be single knuckles. Though some parents opt to leave

[35] Spoiler alert: this might come up again in a future chapter!

such unions alone—it is not absolutely necessary to separate them—my son and daughter-in-law made what I thought was the most humane choice. After all, with only four "fingers" on his right hand he would most certainly have experienced unnecessary goading by other children, stares from curious adults, struggles with activities like keyboarding, and, worst of all in my mind, be relegated to mittens only for the rest of his life!

At the announcement of his impending surgery I did what any self-respecting grandma would do—I offered to fly out to Brooklyn (from Seattle) to console and pamper him. "Are you sure?" my son asked? "We'd love to have you!" I don't know. There must be something about being a grandparent that gives you wings—at least makes you feel like you can—or should be able to—do just about anything for your grandchildren, throwing caution to the wind and agreeing to ten—no make that 21—days of babysitting a 14-month-old, frequently on your own, a mere 9 months after suffering a stroke and being severely limited in getting around. It's not so much forgetting one's limitations at that point; it's more about wanting to believe that one can somehow overcome those limitations whatever it takes in order to do something one has only previously dreamed of doing.

Whatever had possessed me, I now was committed to catching a plane three weeks later to Brooklyn. My son and daughter-in-law offered to help pay for a ticket and emailed to tell me they had found a flight for nearly $400. *Four hundred dollars*?? Surely there had to be cheaper flights out there. A quick internet search on my favorite travel clearing house proffered, as I had expected, several cheaper options, one as low as $300! But then my son dragged me back to reality: "Mom, we were thinking you'd probably want a non-stop flight so you wouldn't have to deal with the hassle of transferring to another plane midway." Oh, right, good thinking. (Obviously more astute—or in tune—than I am!) Back to reality—and higher prices since non-stop flights were only offered by a few airlines—I also began to ponder other concessions that I might need to make. Let's see, four-and-a-half hours sitting upright in a standard coach plane seat could be pretty excruciating. Better pay the extra for not only an aisle but the "even more s p a c e" (as if there are seats with just "more space." Really? That's what you think we believe? If "more space" denotes the seats in which you are relegated, for the duration, to having your knees up to your chin I'd hate to see what the "standard space" option looks like!). Suddenly the $400 tickets turned into $461 with upgrades and taxes. I felt suddenly overly self-indulgent. And it didn't stop there!

I did realize that unless I wanted to arrive at the airport 3 hours before my early morning flight so that I could hoof it all the way from the ticket counter to the gate (which, in my case, is always inevitably the farthest one out from the front door) I would be wise to request wheelchair assistance. So I did. With simply a verbal request. I didn't even have to present evidence that I required one. I asked and *voila*! I would get it! I just wasn't sure exactly how this was going to work but I figured they'd have a plan when I got there.

Then there was the packing. In times past I would plan for a carry-on for a trip like this one but that was clearly out of the question. Oh, well, at least I didn't have to limit myself to 3 oz containers of liquids in a quart-sized Ziploc bag! I would, of course have to carry my purse and computer bag. I wondered what security would be like. Of course, I blithely neglected to consider things like how I would ambulate with my purse, computer bag *and* suitcase from the curb to the ticket counter or how I would manage getting down the boarding ramp to the plane!

As we approached the airport David asked if I would need his help. We were both wondering in this new reality if he would have to park in the garage in order to help me manage my luggage. In the end we concluded that the loading zone police would certainly recuse us for extending our "dropping off" time while he toted my bags inside the terminal and up to the ticket counter, car hazard flashers blinking to confirm that this was not "parking," merely "stopping." This meant I only had to manage all three pieces of luggage up to the actual counter and onto the scale. Then I was directed to some chairs opposite the counter where I would be "called" by my transporter.

I tried not to be offended that my "chauffeur" arrived with one of those "queen-sized" wheelchairs (had the ticket agent mentioned to the dispatcher that "this one would need a bit more room judging the size of her posterior"?!). But then I realized that the extra room in the seat allowed for my computer bag to ride tandem instead on clumsily on my lap. Alright. The agent and the dispatcher were absolved! Now what?

I'm not suggesting that anyone should try to scam the system in order to race to the front of the security line but if you want to get the equivalent of "first class" service without paying the price of the ticket then traveling by airport-issue wheelchair is definitely the way to go! My chauffeur quickly—and not unskillfully—maneuvered my oversized vehicle to the front of the dreaded security checkpoint line, dispatched all of my carry on items to the security belt, and handed me over to the scanner in record time! This is okay, I thought. I mean, if one is going to be handicapped then one should at least get some compensation for it!

Safely on the other side I met up with my chauffer who toted my goods to a bench for me to regroup and then as I turned around I saw her walking hurriedly away with the wheelchair neatly folded together! Crap! Apparently I should have been more specific! I should have said I needed help *all the way to the gate*! Okay, I thought. I can do this. At least she saved me a lot of time and wear-and-tear by getting me this far. If I had to get myself to my own gate (as I previously had predicted, at the very end of the terminal!) then so be it. Might as well get started.

I was about to move out on my expedition when my chauffer came gliding up to me in a motorized vehicle! Duh! I was going to get help all the way to the gate! She hadn't abandoned me as I had assumed. She might have told me what she was doing when she walked away! No matter. All was forgiven. I would ride in style and comfort the two miles to gate 10! (Okay. It's not really two miles but it might as well have been for a gimp!).

I have never been cold in an airport. But a convertible traveling at 3 MPH can create quite a breeze! Good thing I had put my coat on first! Of course, there's another downside to traveling by gimp-coach: you are at the mercy of your chauffer. That is to say, no stops for you! No grabbing a quick Starbucks triple-grande, soy latte; no dawdling or gawking at the booksellers; no bathroom breaks! Just get in, sit down, shut up and hold on! But as a gimp you discover daily that your personal options are limited to a great extent by either your own physical handicaps or the need to depend on others for even the most basic functions. And in this case that also meant being deposited in any seat of her choosing, no time to scout out the possible best option.

May Day

As I was sitting there waiting for the boarding call I observed a more elderly—and I'm happy to say more, shall we say, *portly*—woman slowly inching her way *past* my gate to the only one further out, walking about as fast as I do. Why didn't she avail herself of that wonderful chauffer service offered free by the airport (although they will take a tip, thank you very much!)? Perhaps she was too proud? Not me. Have pretty much lost my pride. Then the convertible cart arrived again transporting an elderly couple and luggage. I found myself watching, judging just how deserving they were of such treatment. Hmmm...let's see...no canes, no crutches. They did seem to be a bit slow but seemed perfectly capable of getting down off the cart without assistance. Okay. Maybe they were just old-age slow. I guess that counts. Another convertible arrived driven again by my chauffer. She grabbed the luggage and looked unsuccessfully for any available seats for the pair of passengers. None being found she circled around once more and encountered a gate attendant who motioned them all up to the ticket scanner and early boarding! Hey, wait a minute I thought! I need extra time and help *too*!! What about me? Then I thought, surely they would call for pre-boarding of passengers who needed some extra assistance, wouldn't they? But while I contemplated this several fully ambulatory passengers took the early boarding of the gimps as a signal that general boarding would begin soon and they raced to get in line! Feeling a sense of panic and envisioning myself being trampled in my clumsy efforts to get to my seat I started toward the line. The word "pre-boarding" was never uttered. Before I got to the end of the now growing line the gate agent called for general boarding of the first few rows! Surely they will see me struggling and give me some assistance right? Not so. I managed to get to the ramp on my own but then realized that I would be holding up the more ambulatory traffic clamoring behind me. I hugged the "far right lane," a signal to those behind me that I would let them pass. But no one did, most likely because they didn't want to appear insensitive. I only hoped I wouldn't trip over one of the joints in the ramp. When I approached the door of the plane I saw the first flight attendant and assumed that she would see me struggling and step out to assist me to my seat, but *no*! She watched while I negotiated the step up from the ramp into the plane, past her with my cane, purse, and computer bag to my seat. I could practically "hear" her thinking, "Good for you! See? I knew you could do it on your own without help!"

At the other end, there was another new experience. Instead of jumping up, grabbing my bags and getting ready to merge into the exiting traffic lane, I obediently waited in my seat, as one of those "who need assistance" until I was directed to get up and exit. This time my "ride" was waiting for me at the forward hatch. I was wheeled in comfort (and without as much drama as the first trip) all the way to baggage claim where my "chauffeur" waited for my suitcase to circle around and then wheeled me to the curb. She was even nice enough to offer me the chance to stop at the restroom! All the while I was agonizing over the fact that I had only two choices for a tip in my purse: a $20 bill or about $0.62 in change! Argh! I couldn't spare a whole twenty and so in humiliation I laid my "widow's offering" in her palm and mumbled my sincerest apologies. It provoked the anticipated response: quiet incredulity.

The Spaz (Spasticity)

I learned a new word today. Actually it isn't really new. I've used a variation of the word—as have, I'm sure many of you—most often in a derogatory but endearing fashion in reference to a friend, that word being "spaz" or "spazdic." We use that word to describe someone who is clumsy physically or mentally and probably thinking it is a variant of "spasm." But today I was introduced to "spasticity," described by the National Institute of Neurological Disorders and Stroke (NINDS) as "a condition in which there is an abnormal increase in muscle tone or stiffness of muscle, which might interfere with movement, speech, or be associated with discomfort or pain." And I think this is the root from which we derive "spastic" (not "spazdic") and that leads us to "spas" (not "spahz" but "spăz"). Is that clear?

How did I find this word and what does it have to do with me? Well, when I was graduated *again* from PT we had asked the question again, even after the physical therapist had already offered an unsolicited assessment: if the tone has not improved by now it will likely not. He confirmed again his prior pronouncement. So, okay. That's that. Right??

Remember my footnote in chapter one about the Stroke Treatment Timeline and how they *conveniently* left something out? What they don't tell you, at least right away—and probably not unless you press for more answers—is that the standard, accepted recovery time for stroke victims is a mere 90 day window. In other words, the pros figure that at best, on average, they have 90 days to rehab you and beyond that it's probably hit-or-miss. That's why they shuffled me off to rehab so quickly. Time, it seems with strokes, continues to be of the essence even after initial treatment.

Part of me would like to simply accept "reality" and try to move on with my new body and my new life. And of course part of me fights that tooth-and-a-nail! And *that* part of me starts to listen to people, like my son, who say that accepting that reality is "giving up" and I should definitely *not* do that! And so, I go in search of answers. Which is how I found "spasticity." I had had little success on searches for information on what all of my medical attendants had called "tone." Turns out, "tone" was not simply *tone*; it was "hypertonia." Our friends at Wikipedia define hypertonia as "a condition marked by an abnormal increase in muscle tension and a reduced ability of a muscle to stretch." But wait! There's more! The type of hypertonia that I suffer from is "spastic hypertonia," which " involves uncontrollable muscle spasms, stiffening or straightening out of muscles, shock-like contractions of all or part of a group of muscles, and abnormal muscle tone" resulting from such things as stroke.

What led me to these revelations is that, being a determined miner of information, I kept digging after my initial unsuccessful trials. I decided to go through the back door of my hypertonia medication, Baclofen. I had been told that Baclofen was specifically used to treat for seizures but I wanted to see what "off-label" uses were listed; perhaps I had one of those. That's when I came across spasticity which led back to hypertonia because they somehow work together and now my brain hurts!

My real motivation—what's more important to me than naming my condition—is finding a *cure* for it! And it turns out that whether the problem can be resolved or not is up for debate. I know that medicine is a practice and not the final symphony, but come on! Is hypertonia/spasticity curable or not?! My PT's seem to think "no" after years in the trenches; but several internet sites implied that it could be resolved with continued stretching. The University of Toledo posted that "the most important thing to treat spasticity is RANGE of MOTION[36] exercises with gentle stretching. These often only take 5-10

[36] *Their* all caps, not mine.

minutes and ideally would be done 3-4 times a day, but once is still better than not at all." The National Stroke Association seconds this advice. And in fact, they admonish the reader that failure to follow this advice could cause the spasticity to mutate into...*contracture*! What? It could get worse?? No one told me this! And wait! What are those "range of motion" exercises with "gentle stretching" that I'm supposed to be doing? One site mentioned having a whole team of specialists to assist the patient overcome spasticity but I don't have *anyone* anymore! They've all "graduated" me.

And what exactly do I have again? Is it hypertonia? Is it spasticity? I don't feel so bad in being confused as I actually found an online forum where a medical professional was asking for clarity and the "expert" who responded began with "Different authors often give different definitions for these terms."[37][!!!!!] Another writes that "*Hypertonicity* can be related to *spasticity*, but *hypertonicity* can be present without *spasticity*."[38] [!!!!!]

But wait...then there's "hypertonia"! It appears that hypertonia is used interchangeably with hypertonicity which is often used interchangeably with spasticity! I don't know how anyone keeps this straight. It makes my mind crazy. So, I'm just going to settle for hypertonia. The definition I found for it (courtesy of NINDS) seems the most straightforward: "Hypertonia is a condition in which there is too much muscle tone so that arms or legs, for example, are stiff and difficult to move. Muscle tone is regulated by signals that travel from the brain to the nerves and tell the muscle to contract. Hypertonia happens when the regions of the brain or spinal cord that control these signals are damaged. This can occur for many reasons, such as a blow to

---

[37] www.physiobob.com
[38] www.pediatricservices.com

the head, stroke..." Bingo! And further, according to another Web site, "Hypertonia is caused by injury to motor pathways in the central nervous system..."[39] Ah...the *central nervous system.* Somehow the weight of those words felt like pressure to my chest. The *central* nervous system—the *granddaddy of them all,* as in "central" to everything, as in "damage to" is often irreparable. I had not thought of it in that way before, the fact that the CNS is made up of two parts: the spinal cord and the *brain.* This wasn't just about a simple rewiring around the "bomb site." This stuff is for keeps.

Now before those of you who know me jump in with all kinds of platitudes like, "I won't accept that this is permanent." or "You're a fighter! I know you can overcome this!" or "I know you'll work your way out of this. Just a little more PT..." let me lay a little bit more reality on you. At the NINDS Web site under the section entitled "What is the Prognosis?" there is no mention of hypertonia ultimately *going away.* The best news is for those whose hypertonia is actually caused by Cerebral Palsy, the effects of which "may not change over the course of a lifetime." The only other changes listed are for the rest of us and these are *not* positive changes. The one thing that is clear is this: hypertonia, in its purest form, *is not curable.* Not with physical therapy, not with medication, not even with, apparently, acupuncture. (See the next chapter.) The only thing left to try is Botox which is merely the injection of poison into the *good* muscle to weaken it so it can allow the *afflicted* muscle a fair shot as its "opponent." More on this later.

---

[39] www.sharecare.com

May Day

Pins and Needles

I started acupuncture with an open mind. Really I did. I hadn't thought of it as an option until a friend asked the question, "What about acupuncture?" What indeed. It was probably worth a try since Western medicine appeared to have reached its limits.

My faith faltered a bit when I told my acupuncturist what the problem was and she looked perplexed. She had never dealt with something like this before and she's been poking people for a quite a long time. Great! Once again I'm an anomaly!

But how to approach the "tone" beast? Deal with the afflicted muscles directly? Go for the brain? She asked my body what she should treat.[40] Frankly, I think my body is confused and overwhelmed. Because it just couldn't get it right. I think all the while that she was asking my body it was calling an unreliable "lifeline.[41]" No matter what approach she took, the beast prevailed. I began to lose faith.

Trust me; I really tried to have the right attitude. I *did*! I felt nothing. No change. I began to think, "Dead is dead. Damage to the central nervous system is permanent. There are certain things even Eastern medicine can't fix." I mean, there must be plenty of other people out there who are still paraplegics even after trying acupuncture, reflexology, spiritual healing, meditation, massage, Cranial sacral, faith healing and all the others.

---

[40] Really. She really asked my body and apparently got a response.

[41] From the game show "Who Wants to be a Millionaire." Contestants who were stuck for an answer to a question could "call a lifeline," requesting help from either the audience or someone by phone.

I didn't give up. At least not right away. Probably because she was so determined. Although, there was a "weak" moment about three-and-a-half months into weekly treatments that she mumbled under her breath something like, "I hate to admit this but maybe the Western practitioners are right." But then she kept on trying! She seemed so confident in Eastern medicine and I wanted to feel the same way. It just wasn't happening. I kept thinking I would tell her that I quit but then during treatment she would try or suggest something new and I would hold out more hope.

That's how I ended up trying Bowenwork© therapy. This form of therapy seems to be based on a proverb repeated by Jesus: "Physician, heal thyself," only you replace "Physician" with "Patient." It is brilliant work really—or rather lack thereof. The practitioner does very *little* work. Supposedly your own body does the bulk of it.

This is not a new idea. In many forms of Eastern medicine the theory is that the body has the capability, within itself, to conduct the healing process. It just needs a "jump start" from something like needles, acupressure, dietary changes, massage, and the like. In my case it seems that there is just a dead battery and no hope of getting it started again. Must be damaged, i.e. a corroded cylinder, or just plain dead. Or maybe it's the alternator. Or the starter.

Grateful and Shit

I hope that the title of this section does not offend. But it is a quote from my friend, Kelly, with whom I was having a discussion recently. I was talking to her about the reality of the "driving" option and how expensive it would be for someone who just isn't ready at this point to drive. Then I got off on a diatribe about how frustrated I get with the responses from some who tell me that I shouldn't feel a certain way or "settle." We groaned again about how people feel the need to cheer you up by saying how lucky you are that you got the use of _____ __________________ (fill in the blank) back, how it could have been so much worse. "Like that's supposed to make it better, like you're not supposed to focus on what you've lost, like you're supposed to be 'grateful and shit!'" she blurted.

Well said, my friend. Well said.

Any Excuse to Get Presents!

In our little beach community, among our closest friends, we have developed this habit of getting together for meals, wine, laughter, tears, wine, catching up, wine, special occasions, and more wine on a somewhat weekly basis on Wednesdays. Each of us takes a turn hosting the "event" in our homes. It is sometimes as simple as "bring your favorite appetizer" or as grand as a theme party such as Cinco de Mayo with all the trimmings. Sometimes we celebrate another's birthday; at times we have spent the time comforting each other in loss. Most often, it is simply an excuse to reconnect in the midst of our busy lives.

Upon my return from Brooklyn I learned that my husband had signed us up to host the following week to *celebrate*!

"Celebrate?"

"Yes, to celebrate your anniversary!"

Ah, yes. My *anniversary*. As if it was a new possession. *My* anniversary. The next Wednesday after my return just happened to fall on *my anniversary*. "Wow, honey. Celebrating my stroke?"

"Not celebrating your *stroke*! Celebrating that you survived it and that you've made such good progress!"

I winced. His face fell.

"No, honey. That's fine. It was very nice of you to think of doing that, of hosting a party in my honor. Thank you very much. What a lovely idea."

I think I might have mentioned before that I *hate* being the center of attention. Really I do. I hated enduring people's rapt gaze while I opened bridal shower gifts or baby shower gifts. I really hate surprise parties! I don't want to be the *reason* for any event!

But he looked so crestfallen. He thought it was a kind gesture and that I'd be pleased that he even conceived such an idea. And I *was* and it *was*. Sigh. It would be fine.

I have a standard response to friends who announce as they age that they just aren't going to celebrate any more birthdays (as if not going through the ritual will somehow slow or abort the aging process? As if!). My retort has always been, "I'll keep having birthdays as long as I keep getting gifts." I mean, as long as you have to keep barreling down that inevitable highway you might as well have fun!

It turns out that in addition to birthdays, wedding anniversaries, and major holidays, stroke recognition days are also great excuses to give gifts. And my friends were only too happy to oblige. Everything from candles to roses and even *jewelry*! Well, if that's the way it's going to be, bring on those "anniversaries"!

May Day

Reluctant Hero

"Thank-you for your words of hope...I think your spirit is stronger than mine...You have amazing strength and faith...I so admire your perseverance...Your journey and the beautiful way you describe it with the joy and the pain gives all of us strength to look at life a little differently...You put me to shame. You are one impressive lady...You are an inspiration...You are an incredible power house of love and faith...your honest and thoughtful sharing--teaching and humbling all of us every day...You are simply amazing, I am so amazed by your fortitude!!...You never cease to amaze me...You are an incredibly strong woman...Your positive and uplifting attitude in the face of such obstacles is inspiring to the rest of us!...let's Celebrate that you are brave to show that you are afraid. That is what heroes do. They are not fearless, they work with fear...and to repeat what many have said, "You are an inspiration to us all"...you are a hero in my book...You are an inspiration to so many as I read what you post and others post. I know you have inspired me!...You are my hero too!...I'm so inspired by your humor and tenacity...You are my Hero!...You amaze me!...You are a real inspiration in the face of adversity...you're my hero!...Thank you God for Anna, whose strength, resilience, courage, determination, humor and love have humbled and inspired us all.[42]"

For the record, I never set out to be a hero. I never really had any heroes myself and don't generally put a lot of stock in the concept. There are people that I have admired or looked up to but I don't recall thinking of them as my hero.

I mean, what *is* a hero really? I put that question to my old friend, Google, and she led me to the site for the Heroic Imagination Project (HIP. It's amazing what you can find online!). According to HIP, heroism is comprised of four elements:

---

[42] Comments from my CarePages Blog

1. It is engaged in voluntarily.

2. It provides a service to one or more people in need, or the community as a whole.

3. It involves potential risk/cost to physical comfort, social stature, or quality of life.

4. It is initiated without the expectation of material gain.[43]

So let's see how I measure up:

1. Well, are we talking about the actual event that catapulted me into supposed heroism? Because unless you are one who believes that we subconsciously bring on our own afflictions, I did not *choose* to have a stroke. Or are we talking about my response, i.e. approach to recovery? I guess I could have refused to engage but that didn't seem prudent. I mean I *did* want to regain physical use of the right side of my body. That part was, I guess, "voluntary." I can't say I *volunteered* for the activities of physical and occupational therapy. Remember that at heart I'm not big on exercise and therapy required a lot of it! But I believed it would help me achieve my goals and, well, I didn't have much else to do while being incarcerated at the Hotel Pacific Providence. So I think the vote would be overall: no.

2. Hmmm...provided a service to folks in need? What was that exactly? Well, many people were purportedly *entertained* by my hospital journal but could we say that in fact that was some sort of *service*? Some folks actually said that they were inspired by my supposed dedication

[43] http://heroicimagination.org/

to the physical therapy. I don't know. Wouldn't just about anybody be dedicated to getting better? How is that heroic? Other folks were moved by my emotional response which was more often than not humorous. They saw this as a heroic rejoinder to my physical calamity. But I don't know that one could argue that that was a "service to one or more people *in need*." Count number 2 as a "no" as well.

3. The risk/cost question. There was certainly a great deal of both when it came to the involuntary event that catapulted me into supposed heroic status. Perhaps that is not the question here. Then are we talking about my response to the event (both physical and emotional) or the fact that I inflicted the details of both on an unwitting public? Again, at least when it came to the physical response there was a great financial cost but I'm not sure that is what HIP means in the use of the word "cost." And the risk of *not* doing physical or occupational therapy was far greater—at least to me—than *doing* it. And I don't think anyone could argue that my emotional response was a risk (unless I might have risked a comedic career by writing bad comedy, i.e. stupid puns) and certainly there was no *cost*. Vote on number 3? A definite "no"! Which leads us to...

4. Well, glory be! I might have scored on this one alone! I mean, I sort of hope (okay, I hope against hope!) that I receive "material gain" from selling this book. However, I don't think any jury could find me guilty of "initiating" my own stroke with the "expectation" of material gain.

Even heroes should receive some compensation for their troubles.

So, okay, I garnered a 1 out of 4 on the hero scale. I don't think that counts. And anyway, in spite of what Mike Dilbeck, Founder & President of the ResponseAbility® Project writes on his Web site on the subject of heroes, (to wit: "Now, truth be told, we all want to be heroes.")[44] I am uncomfortable with that moniker and don't like the attention and expectation implicit in it. I prefer a quiet life of anonymity. Except, I do want to sell my book.

When I Look at the Sea I Imagine all I *Can't* Be

When you live at the beach it is nearly impossible to avoid filling your home with all things nautical. We have jars of beach glass and shells and shelves lined with "interesting rocks," "cool driftwood," and other inspiring finds. We have the commensurate number of nautical items such as a ship's wheel, an antique diving helmet, multiple paintings, photos and ceramic interpretations of lighthouses, antique ship lights, porthole windows, poetry and essay books on the sea, and brass ship plaques. We have dishes, glassware, serving pieces, frames, and table linens sporting fish, shells, and ocean themes. Our deck comes to a point like the prow of a ship and is complete with a ship-like railing, mini ship's wheel and mermaid-inspired maidenhead. Our American flag pole is festooned with nautical flags as well. And then there are the decorative, inspirational signs. These include, "Seaside Treasure" (adorned with shells); "Near the sea we forget the days;" "I love the beach; the ocean makes my butt look smaller," and then my favorite (or at least it used to be): "When I look at the sea I imagine all I can be." I say "used to be" because things are different now.

Now, nearly every day, I realize something else I *can't* do. Hobbling down the beach (yes, yes, I *know*! At least I can do *that*!) with David one morning we were reminded of one of our trips abroad and shared a happy memory. Then I thought—and at the same time he

[44] http://raproject.org/blog/entry/what-really-is-a-hero-anyway

verbalized—good thing we did all that traveling when we could. "There's no way you could get around Delphi now," he observed. Good point. Couldn't haul those suitcases, running across the tracks in Italy to reach our train before it takes off. Couldn't climb those falls in Jamaica. Couldn't line dance with the rest of the passengers on the cruise boat.

When I look at the sea now I feel old and tired, perhaps more so than I should in my early fifties. I am slower and my leg certainly has a lot to do with that. But something else has changed. Even though from outward appearances I give the impression that I'm all back to normal, something is different. It's hard to put my finger on it. When I try to verbalize it people jokingly retort that that comes with menopause or that they have the same problems with aging. But even though this is my first experience of menopause this feels like something else. People say I seem like I'm practically fully recovered but they don't know what's hidden beneath. Sometimes I want to shout: "You have no idea!" I've lived in this body for 54 years now. I know it pretty darned well. Or at least I used to. The truth is, *I don't know who I am any more.*

All I know now is that I have to lower my expectations. And that is something I'm not used to doing. As my husband is fond of saying, I "always go for the A+." And truth be told, everyone else has come to expect that from me as well. Not that I am pressed by others so much but because I come across as the same old me they assume that I *am* the same old me. "Can't" is more a part of my regular vocabulary now.

Up With the Good, Down With the Bad

I've never thought as myself as a good strategist but that's what I'm called upon to do when I'm walking, especially places like the beach. Nearly every step I take must be planned, orchestrated, and engineered. At least if I want to remain upright.

I've got "going up and down stairs" pretty well. You get into a rhythm. "Up with the good; down with the bad." Or in other words, when going *up the stairs or a step* you lead with the working foot; when going *down the stairs or a step* you lead with the non-working foot. I don't know why this works but it does. And I can do it now almost without thinking.

But walking in "the real world" isn't quite as cut and dried.[45] Out there, where the steps aren't neatly laid out with equal measurements in rise and step, I have to spend a lot more time planning my next step—literally. It's like living a chess game (and I've never even *played* chess!); one wrong move and it's checkmate.

First of all, one must judge the height of the potential step up. As I've said, stairs built to code are one thing but that wooden groyne[46] is quite another. I have to decide if I can take that step up with only a cane or walking stick and whether that "bad" knee will bend enough to drag the "bad" foot up. That's only part of the strategy. I also have to judge if I will be able to take the groyne in one step using my "bad" step to hurdle it and land down on the other side. If not, I have to determine if there will be enough space on the top of the groyne for both feet to land safely so that I can then deploy the "down-the-stairs" rule to continue.

---

45 Michael Quinion at www.worldwidewords.org reports on this well-used phrase: "Though we can't prove it, the saying is almost certainly from the cutting and drying of herbs for sale…The first known use of the expression is in a letter to a clergyman in 1710 in which the writer commented that a sermon was "ready cut and dried", meaning it had been prepared in advance, so lacking freshness and spontaneity. The next recorded use is in a poem by Jonathan Swift in 1730 which speaks of "Sets of Phrases, cut and dry, / Evermore thy Tongue supply" — clichés, in other words."

46 Also known as "groin." I choose to use the European spelling which is less suggestive. These are structures—usually wooden or concrete—that lay on the beach stretching out from the land to demarcate property and capture sand.

Then there are the rocks. Can I find a space between them that is large enough to plant a foot or can I find one in my next step that is flat enough (and not too slippery with algae) to land on? I always walk the same direction on the beach and have learned which groynes I can master and which ones I must walk around. I used to walk the beach head down to find beach glass; now I do it out of fear of falling.

The beach isn't the only minefield. Pretty much anywhere I go I have to "think-walk." And it's amazing how many places—from friends' homes to parking lots—have steps with no railing. When I could really walk I thought nothing of skipping up two or three steps without the aid of a handrail. But times are different now and walking up into my favorite little local dress shop without a person to lean on is, well, impossible. I realize that I cannot go a great many places now *alone*.[47]

And some places I must consider whether I can go—*alone* or *not*. In February this year I was invited to join girlfriends on a "girl's weekend" at one friend's family cabin in the mountains. I was ecstatic! I would love to go! Until I came to my senses. What was I thinking? How was I going to maneuver through snow? What if the terrain was impassible for me? And what was I going to do while the rest of the gals went out to play in the snow? Wow…that would be so fun—perhaps scary in unfamiliar surroundings--to be left alone!

In fact, I realize almost daily that I could never function completely alone again. I cannot climb a ladder or step stool; I cannot crouch down to retrieve something that has rolled under the furniture. I cannot carry groceries—or much else—*down*

---

[47] Which is another reason why driving is frivolous. If I could drive myself somewhere how would I be sure I could get around there alone?

the steps to the house and I cannot carry much that won't fit in my little straw basket *up* the stairs. Completely alone—translated "self-sufficient"—is not possible for me now.

Flying Solo

Having just written that, I know...I've made progress. Fourteen months ago I could not walk at all, much less alone. Now after a special planning session with my husband I am allowed to walk the beach alone (that is to say, with my dog, my cane and my mobile phone). I know exactly how to get down the bulkhead steps using both the funky driftwood railing and my trusty walking stick. I'm learning, as I have said, to know the best route over the sand and rocks and groynes. I know how far I can walk (not nearly as far as before) before I must turn back in order to have enough energy and muscle strength to make it.

Fourteen months ago I couldn't shower alone, turn over in bed by myself or close the blinds. I couldn't be *left* alone. Yes, I've made a lot of progress. But "flying solo" isn't always what it's cut out to be.

Recently we were invited to a wine tasting and dining event. It was buffet style which is awesome in that you get to choose what you want from a wide variety of tasty options. But it also meant carrying your own food-laden plate from station to station, walking over uneven turf (it was outdoors) and balancing a wine glass to boot. Needless to say, it was *not* one of the things I can now do. Which meant that my hubby had to do it for me. And naturally the other guests who were with us were off getting their food as well.

May Day

I was alone, again. But not in a good way. It was the aloneness in which you start to feel sorry for yourself and wish that you had at least brought a book so that you could look otherwise occupied and not just conspicuously *alone*.

Left with just my cell phone my options were to browse Facebook or write (I don't play games.) so I wrote a litany of "hates":

> *I hate: needing someone to get my plate at the buffet while I sit at the table alone.*
>
> *I hate: needing help to get in and out of the boat.*
>
> *I hate trying to look nice & feeling like Quasimodo.*

I have a lot of time now to sit and think alone.

Walk, Can't Run

Remember those dreams where you want to run from something scary but you can't? I haven't had one in a very long time but now I feel like the dream has come true. I mean, walking in itself is a challenge; running is out of the question. It's something I never really thought about before: what do people who have mobility issues do when faced with a dangerous situation?

I was finished with one of my acupuncture appointments early one day and I had sent Kyle to the store while I was there. So I texted him that it was such a nice afternoon, I would start walking in the direction of the store and meet him halfway.

We live near a small town surrounded by farms and dairies and it was through this town that I was walking. It's pretty typical of small towns built in the latter part of the 19th century that lacked much industry and so has not grown or changed much. The commerce areas are split up into clusters and even though there are sidewalks connecting the clusters, most of these sidewalks go largely unused. Driving is the preferred form of travel.

Needless to say, I was an oddity not only because of my awkward gait but simply due to the fact that I was *walking*. And I was definitely alone. But I could get over that and the fresh air and exercise would do me good.

Or so I thought. About the time I hit a particularly isolated spot (empty shops separated by empty lots and little traffic at all) I spotted a solitary vehicle making its way down the street toward me. I try really hard not to "profile" people but in my current, vulnerable state it was challenging not to wonder. It was an older gas guzzler—not necessarily a “junker” but it definitely had some miles on it—and it was peopled by a couple who seemed to be in their late 30's/early 40's. What if, I thought. What if they had ill intent? I would be unable to run or protect myself.

As I was pondering this potentiality the car began to slow and get nearer the curb. Keep walking, I told myself. Walk as fast as you can and look straight ahead. Don't give them eye contact. Maybe they are braking for another reason.

The car got slower until it stopped right alongside me. Horrors! My worst nightmare come true! I want to run but I can't! Just keep walking, looking straight ahead. The window rolled down. The woman poked her head out. "Excuse me."

Excuse me? Hmmm...would a person/persons with ill-intent be so polite? "Could you tell us where the clinic is?"

May Day

I felt like such a heel. They were only asking directions! I gratefully steered them in the right direction and soon after they left I saw Kyle coming in our car.

Safety is one thing. Being of use in a hazardous situation is another. Walking the beach alone one day with my dog I was on the lookout for the seal pup that my daughter had reported hearing barking that morning. Our beach is prime harbor seal nursery location; mother seals will leave their pups on the beach while they go out hunting in the bay. Presumably the pups are safer on the shore than in the water with mom though this seems not to be the case.

I had been witness to the violent demise of a very young pup a few weeks before. I had seen it earlier in the day, laying nearly lifeless near some big rocks, waiting for its mother's return. Later in the afternoon my daughter and I started down the beach to check in on him but when we got within eyesight of the rocks we watched with repulsion as three bald eagles descended on him and made him their lunch. While I know that this is the way of nature I was hoping not to experience a repeat with this other pup.

Sure enough, in a short while I heard him "barking" and saw his little head bobbing in one of the channels of water left at low tide. He was calling for his mother. At the same time a neighbor's unattended Golden Retriever bounded out on the sand spit nearby, frolicking with another dog- friend in the early morning sun.

The baby seal barked and bobbed again. And from a distance I was horrified to see the Retriever leap into the channel, diving for the pup. He picked the pup up in his mouth, flung it around and dropped it back into the water. Then he dove in again after it, the pup barking in fear.

In another time I would have run with all my might to stop this brutality but now I looked on helplessly. There was no way I could run to make up the distance of several yards to rescue the pup. I almost turned and walked away. But I could not. Instead I wobbled as quickly as I could across the soft wet mud and algae-slimed rocks, yelling and whistling to the dog, trying desperately to reach my destination without falling and having my own emergency while the dog dragged and tossed the helpless pup like a chew toy.

I managed to reach the pair and send the dogs away. Through a series of phone calls by friends the seal pup was eventually rescued by a wild animal rehab group but in the end, we were told, he succumbed to his injuries.

Of course it is very possible that with that first bite the pup was fatally injured but I can't help thinking that if I could have *just run* to reach him sooner I might have saved him.

Not long ago I had a visit from a good friend who was in town on business. It was great to see him and particularly nice to have company as I had spent most of the day alone. We talked of many things—of course mostly about my condition—and I shared with him this new observation that having impaired mobility makes me more vulnerable.

As he was leaving, stepping out and pulling the door closed he said, "Lock the door after I leave.

Life as a Gimp

The Princess Pass

There's a charming little phrase I've seen printed on towels and decorative signs that goes, "You never know how many friends you have until you buy a beach house." This is also true, I think, of being in possession of a disabled parking placard.

I'm not naming names here or coming to conclusions but some of my family and friends seem absolutely giddy when taking me somewhere over the fact that I have this magic little piece of blue and white plastic that grants special privileges, namely the permission to park up close—and in some cases, for free. And every time I climb into the car to embark on a trip that will lead to parking I get asked the same thing, "Do you have your parking permit with you?" Seriously, if one more person asks me that I'm gonna backhand 'em! Yes, yes, yes already! I have my stupid placard. I have my stupid placard. Don't I always have my placard? Have you even known me in the last 14 months to *not* have my placard with me? Geez! You'd think that *they* were the ones with the disability! Like they just couldn't handle actually walking a few more feet!

I mean, I will admit that it does come in handy but it also carries that old stigma with it: disabled person aboard. Person-with-inability-to-walk- independently-who needs constant supervision and-must-abide-the-constant-refrain-"do-you-need-help?" parking here. Frankly I think the people who really should have to display that placard are the ones who apparently have a *parking* disability! You know the type. They can't seem to stay between the lines or they park so close you have to suck your stomach up against your spine to wedge in or out of your car!

And while we're on the subject...some disabled parking *spaces* have their own disabilities! I mean, those of us with physical disabilities that prevent us from walking well—or far—are most likely afflicted from the waist down, meaning that getting in and out of the car can be a chore. And yet, we parked in one on-street handicapped spot which was alongside a regular curb with no curb cut for wheelchairs or those of us with stepping-up issues. The closest curb cut was down the street a full block at the corner!

Other spaces are no wider than (and side-by-side like) non-handicapped spaces meaning that you not only have to focus on how in the heck to get that knee bent enough in order to get your foot out the door but you have to mind that the door doesn't open so wide that it scrapes the car next door! And can I just say that places like hospitals and rehab centers should triple the number of disabled parking spaces they have? I mean, seriously, if you are going to look for a place where we disabled folks are going to hang out in large numbers it's most likely going to be the rehab center more than the local Target store!

Anyway, as handy as that little placard might be at garnering primo parking places and new friends, it still is a stigma symbol. Unless I rethink it the way my friend did recently who called it my "princess pass." That's right! It's not a *stigma* symbol, it's a *status* symbol! It's my pass because I'm the princess and require royal treatment and special privileges. Yeah! I'm the Princess! Outta my way! Now, if it could only be re-created in a lovely shade of pink!

May Day

Running the Cardio Health Playbook

I really like my doctor but frankly sometimes she really frustrates me. I suppose this is to be expected in a relationship after 15 years; the partners begin really annoying each other.

One of the things that exasperates me is that every time I see her she insists on implying that my stroke was caused by my raised cholesterol, blood pressure and weight (which has been proven untrue!). I am *not* to blame for my current state. I did not contrive this blip in my brain. Besides, if there is any blame to be placed, the finger would be pointed squarely at *her*! After all, *she's* the one who told me at my annual checkup when I had turned the big 5-Oh: "I want to be really careful about your health moving forward. I can't tell you how many women turn 50 and drop dead of a heart attack." Wow! She should be a motivational speaker. Clearly she jinxed me.

Perhaps, secretly, she's happy that my stroke happened because it "proved her right" or at least helps build a case for her continued prodding about tests and pharmaceuticals and supplements and trips to specialists.[48] And she appears absolutely giddy when a specialist agrees with her judgment, which is why she pressed me to get a second opinion from another cardiologist about my taking a statin drug.

My established cardiologist was too laid back about the whole thing apparently. He wasn't ready to jump off that bridge yet. So I obediently went to see the new one.

I was pleasantly surprised. She was friendly, approachable, even self-deprecating. And while she did recommend a statin

---

[48] Of course I don't *really* believe this. But still…

given all my factors she was confident that a low dose would suffice, and that losing 10-15 pounds would perhaps eliminate the need to take them at all. She recommended the South Beach diet, a goal of walking 10,000 steps a day, and perhaps a "cardio exercise workup" to determine my optimal exercise rate—in other words, she was using the new cardio playbook. It's the latest trend in that field of medicine. I left feeling somewhat encouraged and ready to meet the challenges.

First things first. The South Beach diet is all about lots (and I mean *lots*) of vegetables (fine by me!) and protein but less carbs and fruit. I jumped in with both feet (and David volunteered to join me). So we loaded up on veggies and low fat protein options.

Then I bought a pedometer. Easier than trying to count my steps I thought, especially with my compromised memory. In case you've never used one of these handy gadgets, let me explain how it works.

After you get help from your Gen Y daughter on how to turn the gizmo on and reset to zero, you take ten steps and measure the distance you traveled. This determines the size of your personal *gait*. Then you divide 10,000 by the number of steps you took and that gives you the number of 10-foot stretches you need to cover. Let's see in 10 steps I covered 10 feet. A little quick calculation...divide this, multiply that...I would need to walk 10,000 feet a day or 1.893 miles. That should be easy enough—between my dog-walking routine and just going up and down the stairs...I racked up a total of...about *half* that! And that's on a good day!

May Day

The problem with running the same playbook for everyone is that it doesn't necessarily take into account physical *ability*. I simply *can't* walk that much!

No worries, I thought. I can make it up by using my "new" stationary bicycle. But the next day, walking barefoot (as I do in the house) at a quick (for *me* anyway) clip, my foot swinging out to the right as it does since I can't bend my knee enough I *slammed* my foot right between the pinky toe and it's neighbor against a door jamb. (Yes, it is appropriate for you to cringe in empathetic understanding.) It hurt like you-know-what! But even more importantly, the collision appeared to have broken my pinky toe rendering me totally crippled for a day or two and unable to wear closed-toe shoes (necessary for, among other things, using the stationary bike) for six weeks!

On top of that, the diet ceased to work after the first three days and for weeks after I started I stayed firmly at a total of five pounds lost! So much for the cardio playbook.

Which leads me to this point: people tend to forget that I can't operate again as normal, assuming I can do the usual stuff like a healthy, non-handicapped person. I don't blame them; I have trouble remembering myself sometimes. Like, "sure, I'll be happy to do...no wait, there's no *way* I can do that!" Happens nearly every day.

In Defense of Depression

I know that by now many of you—at least the ones who have suffered a life-changing, game-changing tragedy—are wondering: "Is this woman always so upbeat?" And the answer is no. Let me tell you, it happens more frequently than I admit. But in case you haven't noticed, other people don't handle the "negativity" so well. They don't know what to *do* with it. So at best they try to talk you out of it. It's as if we're all programmed to cheer each other up, even if we are unfamiliar with the circumstances.

To wit, the other day I met the friend of a friend. Of course, as is the case these days, *my* friend felt the need to *explain* me. And I get that. I really do. I'm different now. I need explaining. Anyway, her friend's response was pretty typical too ("I'm so sorry; you're so young, etc."). Then her friend offered to help me and my glass of wine down the stairs to the dining table outdoors. As we walked (well, *she* walked; *I* did that *other* thing that I do) down the stairs she must have felt compelled to break the silence or else the need to cheer me up (?) because she exclaimed, "You're doing so well!" I don't think—and I'm pretty sure she knew—that she had any real reference point from which to make that observation. She just *had* to say something positive. It's what we do.

Well, I'm here to say that depression (not the clinical kind that truly debilitates for which some, including *me,* take medication[49] but rather the garden variety, occasional blue mood) is *really okay*. I don't believe that anyone completely escapes the doldrums. Even Pollyanna had her moments. It's a fact of life. Depression *happens.*

The thing is other people just don't know what to do with your down mood. It's very much like not knowing what to do with a personal loss. We have to say something but what can we say? Surely we can't say something like, "Yeah, wow, what has happened to you *really sucks!*" It just wouldn't be right, wouldn't be

[49] There, I said it. The gig's up. I take anti-depressants!

proper. We don't want to get down in the pit with the depressed so we stand up above and offer pithy platitudes.

I'd just like to say here and now that depression is just as much a human emotion as happiness and just because it makes us uncomfortable to be around a depressed person doesn't mean that *that* emotion is one that needs fixing any more than a "pleasant" emotion does. So what do you *do*? What do you *say* to a depressed person? Years ago when David and I were taking classes to become Stephen Ministers[50] the instructor shared an image of the perfect answer. When we see someone in despair we say they are "in the pits" and we can respond one of three ways: 1) we can climb down into the pit with them but now we're both down there without a rope. Not very helpful. And now we're depressed too! or 2) we can stand up above (sympathy) and shake our heads and wring our hands and offer clichés of pity. Also not very helpful; or 3) we can plant our feet firmly on the ground above and offer a hand up when the person is ready to climb out (empathy).

In the meantime, it's okay not to try to "talk them out of it." As Meg Ryan, playing "Kate" in the movie "Forget Paris," said to her estranged fiancé, "Charlie," in response to his sadness: "Go ahead. Swim in it...til your fingers get all pruney."

I have good news and bad news. The good news is that I'm climbing up out of the hole. The bad news? I can see the light but some days it's pretty dim.

---

[50] "To put it simply, a Stephen Minister is a Christian who has been through an official training under the auspices of his or her church to learn how to walk along side a person going through a normally temporary crisis and be there for him or her." http://wannabwriter.hubpages.com/hub/Should-You-Become-A-Stephen-Minister

Rewired

Remember how early on in the book I talked about the "creeping paralysis" that had taken place that fateful day? Strangely, a year later I have noticed an odd physical event: sometimes I'll have a persistent itch either at the joint where my right leg joins the abdomen or actually up on the right side of my abdomen and when I scratch it, my right leg and foot twitch and jump. It is as though they have some bizarre new connection.

Years ago an employee of the phone company came to our neighborhood to do some work on the phone lines. About an hour after he left, my phone rang. The caller had the wrong number but what was weird was that she was attempting to reach one of my neighbors. Odd coincidence I thought. A while later the phone rang again. Another wrong number. Another caller looking for *the same neighbor*! And then it happened again! A coincidence? Turns out that in fact while disconnecting and reconnecting our phone lines the phone company lineman had plugged them in *backwards*! I wonder if that can happen in the brain.

And why is it that my brain can work around some damage (I can use my hand and arm normally again) but not other damage (i.e. this darned leg!). I made an appointment to see my stroke neurologist.

At the doctor's office, after catching up, we pulled out the old photo albums and reminisced about my stroke. I wondered aloud why I had managed to regain use of my upper extremities and looking at my "pictures" he noted a plausible explanation: my brain had apparently reached the limits of its capabilities. (Not the first time, mind you. I've had that experience frequently over the years. Especially when it came to algebra.)

It seems that my cavernous malformation[51] is located along the left frontal lobe's "motor speedway" (or for those of you brainiacs, the corpus callosum). According to the Oregon Health and Science University Brain Institute (my italicized comments added), "The corpus callosum (Latin for "tough body" —*ironic, isn't it? Not so tough as you thought you were, huh mister?*) is a broad, thick bundle of nerve fibers in the entire nervous system, running from side to side and consisting of millions and millions of nerve fibers. (*not just millions, but millions and millions!)* If we cut a brain in half down the middle, (*Why would ANYONE do that??!!*) we would also cut through the fibers of the corpus callosum." (*Duh!*) I prefer the motor speedway image.

The corpus callosum is in the middle of the brain just above the brain stem running, basically, front to back. Just a smidge above that is one end of the primary motor cortex which runs side to side perpendicular to the corpus callosum up over the cortex. Are you with me here? This primary motor cortex is otherwise known as the "homunculus" or Latin for "little man." The homunculus is called that because it—sort of—resembles a little man lying on his stomach with his head twisted around facing outward, as if over a large round rock, only this guy is

[51] Did I mention before that months down the road from my stroke, when we had learned of this little appendage in my brain, my darling husband still thought it was a large hole?

draped over the motor cortex of the brain. [52] It actually doesn't seem very comfortable, at that.

Anyway, this homunculus is thought of as the "body within the body." As the blog site io9.com puts it, "We all know what bodies look like from the outside. This cortical homunculus is how your brain sees your body from the inside." There are actually two of them, one over each motor cortex. "Every part of the body is represented in the primary motor cortex, and these representations are arranged somatotopically[53]-- the foot is next to the leg which is next to the trunk which is next to the arm and the hand. The amount of brain matter devoted to any particular body part represents the amount of control that the primary motor cortex has over that body part. For example, a lot of cortical space is required to control the complex movements of the hand and fingers, and these body parts have larger representations in M1 (*the homunculus*)[54] than the trunk or legs, whose muscle patterns are relatively simple."[55]

In lay person's terms, this little dude is pretty strange looking! His head and hands are much larger than—and out of proportion with—his legs and feet and correspondingly, the sections of the brain that control those motor functions are also out of proportion. That's because your hands are much more intricate machines than your dumb old legs and feet. To put it in perspective, the sections of the motor cortex that correspond to the feet and toes (each with only one section) are only about a third

---

52 Turns out those brainy folks who studied and named all the parts of the brain that we know something about can be somewhat imaginative as well. It's a little like ancient people seeing a face in the moon.

53 Organized in a point-to-point representation of the surface of the body.

54 My insertion

55 www.brainconnection.positscience.com

as big as those which correspond to the hand, fingers and thumb (each with its own section).

(Can I just say that in researching for this book I have encountered some pretty weird stuff out there on the Internet? For instance, there seems to be a whole community of homunculus followers out there – like some strange cult – who have written about this weird little man, created at least one Facebook page for him, even created animated videos about him. Some people just have way too much time on their hands!)

Anyhoo...all this is to say that upon closer examination of my MRI it seems that the cavernous malformation lays alongside this homunculus on the left motor cortex of my brain. (Remember...the left side of your brain controls the right side of your body. Confusing to say the least!). The bleed must have begun at Homunculus' feet (hence that's where I felt it first) and spread "eastward" past the legs, trunk, shoulder, arm, hand, and fingers stopping just short of my middle and forefinger and thumb. Which explains why those were the only appendages I could move by the time I reached the hospital. Another way to look at this is to imagine a paint can spilling: the paint might pool right at the point of the tip over and then depending on the terrain might spread out from there, getting thinner as it spreads until it finally stops.

What does all this mean? Well, the paint spill started at my foot. That means the greatest part of the spill was there and caused the most damage to my foot and leg. And quite possibly, this damage is just too great[56] for the super muscle known as the brain to fix. In other words, the circuitry there is fried. Specifically, the nerves controlling my peroneus longus and my

---

[56] Or perhaps, not important enough to bother with, as far as my brain is concerned.

flexor digitorum are toast! This renders those muscles weakened and unable to win the tug-o-war with the opposing muscles. Consequently, the outside muscle of my calf that pulls against the inside muscle of my calf allowing me to keep my leg straight when I walk and the bottom muscle of my foot that pulls against the top muscle of my foot allowing me to flex and extend my toes (and wiggle them in the sand) can't pull their weight any more. Of course, there are probably other muscles—and tendons—affected which all-in-all makes "walking" impossible and "getting around" a chore.

The Secret(s)

Oddly enough, most of what I have learned about my condition did not derive from the ready explanations offered up by medical staff. I have had to do the digging and asking. The most recent visit with the neurologist that I just wrote about was not initiated by him; I asked for that appointment specifically to get more answers to lingering questions. Why is this? Why do they seem to *keep secrets*?

I am reminded of a conversation I had years ago with my mother's oncologist. After months of hearing from my parents that my mom was doing a good job of "fighting" her cancer and vague explanations about her real condition I decided to go right to the expert for answers. This was in the days before HIPPA and I was able to have a conversation by phone with her physician. I asked him how my mother was doing and he blurted out, "Your mother is *dying*!" I was stunned! Not once had my parents let on that this was so. How could that be? I put this question to him and then asked if my mother knew about her death sentence. His response was nearly as surprising as the first. "She hasn't asked me," he replied, "And if she hasn't asked me I figure it means that she doesn't want to know. So I won't tell her."

I guess I understand that. I guess. Especially in his line of work where bad news is most likely the norm. I don't know if that is the reason medical professionals don't share or if perhaps they think that the average patient won't understand what they tell them or doesn't care to know. Or maybe they like having their secret jargon stay secret; maybe they are worried that if they reveal the secrets they will lose their status. I just don't get it. And maybe, again, I'm an anomaly in that I *want* to know; I *need* to know. I just find it odd that I have to *ask*. And that I even had to figure *that* out.

Almost Better in So Many Ways

"You're doing so well!" I hear this pronouncement on a regular basis from friends and strangers alike. And, yes, relatively speaking, I *am* doing much better than I did before (not *before* but before. I must differentiate now. There was "before the stroke" or B.S. and there is "after-the-stroke-before-recovery" or B.R. Compared to B.R. I am doing much better. I am *almost better in so many ways.* I can talk, think, and get around. But it's not "just like old times." And from my perspective (and I know mine doesn't seem to count for much, but…) B.S. was a much more preferable time.

It is hard not to feel this way, when I truly allow myself to feel. It's hard not to compare. It's human nature. It's also human nature to spew pithy platitudes like "it could always be worse." Although, it seems that there is some unspoken, unwritten baseline at which we *draw the line* on pithy. I mean, people will tell me that I'm doing so well in my recovery but would they say that if I was permanently in the wheelchair with limited use of my arm? Would they say, "Hey, at least you can sit up"? Would you say to the bereaved husband at the funeral of his wife, "Cheer up! It could always be worse! You could have lost your whole family"?

Yes, I know. It *could* always be worse. But that does not diminish my truth: I am different now. I think differently, I write differently, I get around differently. And the getting around part is the toughest for me to take.

I know, I know...you're thinking: "But at least you *can* get around!" But I think your optimism is falsely based on a presumption that getting around is all that is required. And that the lowly leg and foot are pretty expendable. Does it occur to you that when you can't rely on the strength and maneuverability of the leg and foot that your hands and arms must come to the rescue? They must, in a sense, "step in" and pick up the slack?

This became ever so clear to me years ago when, while playing basketball with my oldest son, I sprained my ankle. Now I know what you're thinking, "Big deal. A sprained ankle. At least you didn't break it." But that sprained ankle rendered me nearly helpless as a mother of four young children (whose husband had just left for a week-long business trip). I could not walk on it, of course, so was constrained to using crutches. But, how do you *use* crutches? With your *hands and arms!* And while your hands and arms are busy being your "working" foot and leg what do you have left for really *doing* anything? I couldn't even carry a cup of coffee to the chair in which I would sit my sorry self. Life's daily activities were nearly impossible without some help. I might as well have broken it.

May Day

The fact of the matter is that when I say that my foot and leg are still affected and don't work it is nearly the same as saying my foot and leg, and at least one—if not both—of my hands/arms, are impaired as well. Whether it's walking up or down stairs or over a groyne or down three steps at a friend's house the action requires one working leg, one tag-along leg, at least one hand holding a cane and often the other holding onto an arm or a wall or a railing. That doesn't leave any appendages for carrying anything. It's not in my nature to walk in to the house from a grocery shopping trip without bringing in at least some of the bags. I'm accustomed to being able to carry the dry cleaning bag down from the bedroom to the car or wrestle the built-in vacuum cleaner hose up and down stairs to clean. And I'm definitely not happy about having to have someone get my food for me at the buffet, as if I'm a small child. But this is my life now.

And for God's sake...*please* stop telling me that "time will tell," "this could still get better," "don't give up—keep working at it," blah, blah, blah! Those tired expressions just aren't helping! At some point you need to just accept certain inalienable facts and figure out how you will adjust to live with them. Pie-in-the-sky-hope-for-a-miracle-thinking can often lead to continued disappointment. There is nothing wrong with living in reality and not spending all your energy on hoping, wishing, and pushing for some cure. It isn't unhealthy to accept and move on. It doesn't mean I'm giving *up* or giving *in*; it means I'm moving *on*.

Yes, it could always be worse. Of course it could. But knowing that doesn't stop one from sometimes being down in the dumps about one's own reality. It's all relative. Most of the time I am just very grateful for having gotten back so much of what was once me. But please allow me those blue moments of remembrance. Things *are* different. And I need time to adjust. And I need time—and space—to grieve.

Birds of a Feather

I am learning to be a gimp. And I mean that in the most complimentary way. There is a gimp brother—and sister—hood and we have to stick together cuz it's a jungle out there! Recently, as I was going through my standard gyrations of stuffing my unwieldy leg into the car, the gimp getting into the car next to us noticed my single point cane and advised me that her new triple point cane with the extra hand grab was really the way I should go. It was much more reliable and gave her more stability. And she advised me to shop for my new accessory online where I was sure to find a great deal.

At a neighborhood BBQ I noticed that the hostess who was a young mother of two was getting around with the help of a permanent leg brace (it looked as though she had had polio) and I wondered with admiration how she did it: how she managed to "chase" after two small children, how she carried them when they were too young to be mobile, and how she also manages to hold down a fulltime job. I was in awe. And I realized that in my previous life I wouldn't have given it a second thought. But now I know what it takes.

Of course, there is definitely competition among us gimps as well, mostly for parking places. I used to be annoyed that it seemed that often the only *available* parking spaces were marked with that ubiquitous little white person in his(?)/her(?)/its(?) wheelchair riding on a lovely field of royal blue. Now I get annoyed that even in parking lots with multiple handicapped spaces these are frequently full. Are there really that many of us out there? I also find myself judging when I'm struggling out of the car and the "handicapped" person next to me seems to be getting around pretty danged well. Hmmmm....I mean there *are* degrees of handicapped.

For better or worse, we are a community. I have been a member of many different groups for many different reasons. I was even a member of the Klutz Club, a tight-knit group of four teen girls who shared much in common but especially a propensity for clumsiness. This is one community that I would just as soon have skipped but here I am. I am a gimp, the ultimate klutz.

It Ain't Over Til...It's *Over*[57]

Lest I had thought that my days of complete reliance on other people were over I am often reminded that, as I quoted in an earlier chapter, "recovery from a stroke is a lifelong process." I thought when I blissfully said goodbye to my wheelchair and then my walker that I truly was finished with those relationships. I was ready to move on. I had gained a lot from them at the time but there comes a moment when you know that you've grown beyond a relationship and you just need to cut the ties.

That is, until you do something utterly stupid and random that sets you back a ways. Two steps forward; one giant leap back. I have frequently bemoaned the condition of my right leg and foot and the fact that I seem to have progressed as far as I will. But I never thought I would *regress* in my recovery. The reality is that this is always a possibility. As long as I have a weak link I will never have a completely strong chain.

---

[57] Yogi Berra, first; Lenny Kravitz, second.

Nearly 15 months into my recovery I rounded a corner too quickly (i.e. I wasn't calculating my *every* step) and my ankle essentially "crumbled." Not as in "the bone crumbled" but metaphorically speaking, the ankle gave way as if it were a cookie crumbling and I tried to stop myself from falling. I cannot be faulted for this attempt; it is quite the human reaction: falling *bad; not* falling *good*!

But as is often the case, while we're attempting to solve one problem we create another, perhaps equally perplexing problem. And in my case, I didn't even solve the initial problem.

It happened so quickly that I am hard-pressed to recall exactly the events that led to me lying on the floor in front of my startled granddaughter trying to catch my breath in spite of the pain I was feeling. I just know that I felt myself falling, tried to grab for anything that would help keep me upright, and, finding nothing, continued my descent to its certain conclusion: the hard floor. I remember that I fell on my right side—smacking my right ankle bone and my right hip—and I remember gently, slowly, rolling over to my back to assess the damage. And I remember thinking: I gotta get up from the floor fast because my husband will be returning shortly from his crabbing outing and if he sees me prone on the floor he's likely to end up there himself! By now my granddaughter had recovered from the shock of seeing her Nana tumble down like a too-tall stack of blocks and decided that Nana in her current configuration presented a whole other prospect for play. She climbed on top of me and straddled my stomach. And she refused to budge! As far as she was concerned, this was no emergency; this was opportunity!

I finally was able to pry her from me and begin the process of getting back to my feet (no easy *feat* these days) and by the time my unsuspecting husband arrived on the scene there was no more scene. I had "righted" myself and was discreetly hiding the fact that I was using my cane *indoors* behind the kitchen island where I blissfully continued kneading my French bread dough. He raced in breathless having only 15 minutes to shower and get out the door for a meeting. "So I've got to go," he blurted, "The water is on to boil and you'll have to put the crab in and cook it for me." "Okay!" I responded feebly, knowing full well that there was *no* way I was going to make it down all the stairs to the bulkhead where the pot was set up but there was also *no* way I was going to let *him* know that! That's what friends and neighbors were for, after all. Besides, I wasn't feeling *that* badly; I was probably just shaken up a bit. This too would pass.

But as the minutes ticked away I knew the ruse was up. I was going to need some help and most likely a ride to the walk-in emergency clinic. I texted David and asked him to call when his short meeting was over and the phone rang almost immediately. "Did you fall?" was his response to my "Hello." Damn! I thought. How did he know that?!

The docs at the clinic couldn't find any broken bones (great news!) but I was still in pretty bad shape. Probably a muscle sprain. But in the weirdest place! Not in my hip or my knee or my ankle. No, this sprain appeared to be in one or more of the muscles that run from the femur toward the inner thigh and also possibly one in my groin! The resulting effect was that as time went on walking became ever more difficult and painful. In fact walking wasn't the only thing that elicited a painful wince. Bending over from the waist, bending at the knee, even ultimately sneezing or moving my leg the "wrong way" in bed would cause one of the muscles to clench it's fist at me for my clumsiness.

I knew by now that my single point cane wasn't gonna cut it for the time being. In an act of utter humility I had to ask for my walker and wheelchair back from a friend who had had to borrow them and had just recently been able to graduate from them herself. Actually, I wanted to refuse the wheelchair but she insisted, which ended up being the more prudent decision. That night I hobbled—with lots of help—upstairs and into bed not knowing when (or if) I would be able to go back down them again. I found myself longing once more for my little trundle bed in the office to which I could retreat without stairs and on which I could rearrange myself easier having the convenience of the bed frame to use as leverage.

Then began a regimen of ice packs, pain killers, muscle relaxants and anti-inflammatories and new strategies to be learned (i.e. how to get up into bed without sending the muscle into spasms; how much weight I could put on my leg without sending the muscle into spasms; how big a step I could take with my right foot without sending...you get the picture.) And boy, was I feeling sorry for myself! I was already reminiscing about how good I had had it just the day before when I could actually walk on the beach albeit with a walking stick and careful steps. At least I could do *that*! Now I couldn't even *get down the stairs* to the beach, let alone walk it. And we had to cancel out of all the social activities we had planned for that weekend. *And* it was a beautiful summer weekend weather-wise and I was stuck *indoors* staring out our big picture windows at the sparkling water and blue sky instead of being *out* in them!

How did this happen? I was asked. But I never answered truthfully. The real truth is that those Puritans who were fond of quoting the book of Proverbs from the Bible were quite literally right: "Pride goeth before a fall."[58] As much as I don't want to admit it, the chances of this happening would most likely have been significantly diminished if I had been wearing my AFO (remember? Ankle-foot orthotic?) And why *wasn't* I wearing my AFO you ask? Because it is *ugly and clunky and demands that I also wear "sensible"* (translated: "ugly") *shoes*. Yes! It's true! I admitted to the fact that I'm willing to take a chance on falling and putting myself back a few steps in the recovery journey for the sake of whatever pride in my outward appearance I might still have. Look, it's bad enough that I am facing the divorce from my beloved shoe collection; can't I at least maintain some shred of dignity with my meager shoe wardrobe of little "ballet" style shoes and flat-soled sandals with sling backs? Gimme a break! (No! Not that kind! You know, the kind of break as in "pause" or "escape.")

The reality is that whether I'm better equipped or not, this will most likely *not* be the last time in this lifelong recovery that I will suffer a setback. The recovery ain't over til…

One False Move...

Looks like the book will be a tad longer. I thought that last chapter was the end of that part of the story but…in the immortal words of a dear friend, "It gets *better*!" Remember how the local ER reported that their x-rays showed no fractures? Well, apparently, you shouldn't believe everything you hear![59]

After two weeks of trying to recover from "a bad sprain" I took myself (well, actually, Kyle took me) to my primary care doc-

---

[58] Actually, truth be told the actual verse in Proverbs (16:18) purports, "Pride goeth before destruction and a haughty spirit before a fall." But as usual in the English language, over time we shortened it.

[59] And they shouldn't believe everything they *read*!

tor. She—supposing that the ER x-rays were accurate—thought the incessant pain in my upper thigh/groin could be caused by a hernia or blood clot. (After her examination I was pretty sure the pain was from her poking around saying, "does it hurt here? Here? Here?). She decided to send me for an ultrasound the next day. I was skeptical, but hey, what do I know?

By the time I left her office I was no longer able to put *any* weight on my leg; nada, zilch, nuttin! I was then confined to the wheelchair and to once again sleeping on the main floor. Hmmm...it was all so familiar, like...déjà vu! I wasn't happy about it but considered the situation temporary so I made the sofa my new center of operations.

We trekked down the next day for an ultrasound. After the technician did her thing, the radiologist stepped in to have a look. They didn't say much but I could tell by their mumbling and looks that hernias and blood clots were not my problem. "So, they took x-rays of your hip at the clinic and said it wasn't fractured?" the radiologist queried. "That's right. They said that it looked fine and that I probably had a bad sprain." "I think we need to do another x-ray," he said with concern.

When he came in to talk to me after the x-ray he announced gloatingly that, in fact, I had a fracture after all and that the next stop would most likely be the ER at the hospital for surgery! He would order a CT first to confirm it. And then he asked me something that didn't really register at the time but struck me later. He wanted to know if I had ever had a bone density test. "Yes," I said. He wanted to know when. "In the last couple of years I think." "What was the result?" he wondered.

May Day

"Osteopenia"[60] I reported.

"Hmmm...you might need to have another test done."

All I was thinking at that moment was: What?? I'd been walking around (okay, more like hobbling!) for two weeks on a *broken hip*?! *And* how did the local ER's x-ray technicians miss that?

The radiologist made phone calls to get me in to an orthopedic surgeon in the area. After a two-and-a-half hour wait, I met with him. He was very personable and helpful. He discussed my x-rays, showing me exactly what had happened: I had fractured the neck of my femur (a femoral neck fracture) but the good news was it was not only that sort of fracture but that the resulting "slump" of the bone head was at a valgus[61] inclination, which is a good thing in orthopedic terms when it comes to a femoral neck fracture. It meant that they didn't *have* to do surgery; surgery was optional to relieve the pain as the bone would heal on its own.

I was still holding a grudge against the local ER clinic and their failed x-ray department. But the surgeon assured me that it was fairly common to miss such fractures, even with the most

---

[60] According to www.health.harvard.edu," Like their names suggest, Osteopenia and Osteoporosis are related diseases. Both are varying degrees of bone loss, as measured by *bone mineral density,* a marker for how strong a bone is and the risk that it might break. If you think of bone mineral density as a slope, normal would be at the top and Osteoporosis at the bottom." I'm somewhere near the bottom.

[61] According to www.wikipedia.com, "In orthopedics, a **varus deformity** is a term for the inward angulation of the distal segment of a bone or joint. The opposite of varus is called valgus." More confused?

trained eyes. He was actually much nicer towards them than I was.[62]

So my options consisted of no surgery and just "physical therapy" which was really just increased weight bearing over time until the bone healed and the pain went away; or surgery which would alleviate some of the peripheral pain. We agreed that I would go home for the weekend, armed with heavy-duty pain pills, and let him know by Monday whether I thought I needed surgery for the pain or not.

By Monday morning it was no contest. I had suffered excruciating pain all weekend and decided surgery sounded like a vacation. So they scheduled me for Wednesday morning. I went in willingly, ready to be pain free. But once I emerged from my anesthesia-induced stupor I recognized an old, familiar feeling—nausea-inducing pain! I wondered if I had just spent good insurance money for nothing. Once again, I went home with even more heavy-duty pain meds along with anti-spasm and nerve pain meds and the accompanying stool softeners to alleviate the constipation caused by those pain relievers. I was a tad disappointed. Had I been duped? I was so impressed that someone who made his living doing surgery had not jumped right at the chance, had actually basically told me I didn't need surgery. But had he sold me a line in order to convince *me* to *choose* surgery?

My answer came a few days later. The pain I had been feeling in thigh, groin, knee and various other places magically disappeared, without pain medications. It was a miracle! But now the new reality set in: I was basically back to where I was a lit-

---

[62] Turns out for good reason. As you will see, X-rays don't always tell the whole story.

tle over a year ago—immobile, confined to the main floor of the house, and dependent on everyone for everything. Damn! I thought I had really left wheelchairs, walkers, four-point canes, PT, OT, bathing with company, and sleeping alone behind me—at least for a few years. How did this happen?

One night before my surgery David asked me how I felt about the upcoming procedure. I said I felt pretty good about it because I was really looking forward to having a lot less pain. And then he observed that it must have been weird—and frustrating—that after the stroke I had finally reached the "new normal," not necessarily exactly where I had hoped to be but at least I knew what I had to work with and was ready to move forward. And then to have something happen that put me right back where I started from a year earlier. I was reminded of the book, "Alice Through the Looking Glass," in which the Red Queen (or was it the White one?) complained of having to run just to stay in one place. One false move, that's all it took.

A few days later, in a repeat of the PT assessment of a year earlier, the PT intake specialist gave me a list of things to remember in handling my hypertonicity: neutral warmth, weight bearing (gee, that sounds familiar), gentle stretching, and slowing down. I am to remember those daily and throughout the day. I suddenly thought about my first encounter with driving a stick-shift: depress clutch, move gear shift, gently release clutch at the same time as gently accelerating. I wondered then how I was ever going to remember to do everything in the right order, at the right time. I suddenly felt like I was learning how to drive a manual transmission again.

The Scarlet Letter(s)

During the first couple of weeks post-surgery I was visited by a nurse whose job it was to remove the stitches, take vitals, double check that I was taking appropriate medications, etc. On one of those visits the nurse asked me *again* about my history—stroke…caused by?...resulting in?...which led to… At which point she paused and pronounced: "You know, you are a fall risk." The words echoed in my head like the clanging of a large bell. "You *ARE* a *FALL RISK*." "You ARE incurable." "You ARE—and ALWAYS WILL BE—damaged goods."

I guess I must have known that but no one had ever made that pronouncement before; no one had actually said aloud that I was forever more, a "fall risk." I imagined a set of red letters emblazoned on my forehead—FR.

Déjà vu All Over again[63]

Four weeks post surgery I had a follow-up appointment at the surgeon's office, which is to say not *with* the surgeon but with his PA. All busy specialists these days have a PA (physician's assistant, aka Dr. Wannabe) or an MA, medical assistant who see patients for the mundane stuff like post-op follow-up. After a couple of minutes of conversation he sent me down the hall to have an X-ray. The X-ray technician asked me to do things that I'm quite sure I wasn't supposed to do like standing without a walker or cane or anything and then facing the X-ray "gun" with my right foot elevated on a stool and turned out (think Marlene Dietrich).

---

[63] Another wonderful Yogi Berra Yogi-ism.

May Day

Back in the exam room the PA looked at my new X-rays. Needless to say I had been expecting all along that this was just a typical routine visit and that he would say, "Yup, things look just fine." But he didn't. With much gravity he pointed to the picture of my screws and, shaking his head, said that he thought they were precariously close to my hip joint and that he wanted to confer with the surgeon. Wait...*what?!*

Sure enough the surgeon confirmed that the screws were too close to the joint and that, (gasp!), I would be facing yet another surgery to replace them! Are you *frikking* kidding me??!

Surgery was scheduled ASAP as encroachment of the screws on the joint itself is a no-no. In the meantime ("in-between time, ain't we got fun?"), the PA had but one warning for me until the surgery: to not move my hip in any of the ways that their X-ray tech had just done! But this time surgery was scheduled in their outpatient surgery center (makes you wonder why the first one had to be an overnight at the local hospital...hmmm...just saying...). Once at the center I was finally able to talk to the surgeon. How did this happen? Why did this happen? The PA had said that it was pretty rare. So what went wrong?

The surgeon offered up three plausible solutions: 1) extra-soft bone tissue; 2) the head of the femur which was compacting down had not finished doing so when they had put in the screws; or 3) the screws were actually farther in than they had thought but due to the X-ray options at the hospital they were unable to see that that had happened.[64] Okay. So, any one of those seemed reasonable. Of course my friend was convinced that they just put in the wrong sized screws because those were

---

[64] Remember what the radiologist said earlier about X-rays?

the size they use on everybody and it didn't occur to them that I might need another size. I like to give people the benefit of the doubt though, so I was prepared to accept one of his explanations.

Back home I continued with my PT. Nearly eight weeks into this new venture I still had only progressed to "walk" with assistance using just a "the weight of the leg" on the offending limb. Two weeks hence I had my first post-second-surgery follow-up appointment with another PA at the surgeon's other office in a brand-new medical building. David took me to the appointment but needed to run to his office a few blocks away to take care of some business. "No worries," I assured him, "If you get me to the elevator I can wheel myself to the office. I have plenty of time."

I sometimes have too much confidence in myself—and in the world around me. No matter how many strides our society seems to have made toward accommodating those who are "differently-abled" we still miss the mark—often in a big way.

I got to the floor where the doctor's offices were without a hitch but once out of the elevator I faced a long trek down a carpeted hallway. Carpeted? Really? What's wrong with hard-surface flooring? Try wheeling yourself manually in a wheelchair down a *carpeted* hallway of any kind of distance and you'll soon know why I ask the question. But uncomplaining, I put on my big girl panties and began the journey.

Halfway there was the door to the restroom. Good idea, I thought, since I'm still early for my appointment I might as well take care of business now. The interior designer got points for choosing a universally-useful lever-type handle but when I backed up to the door to use my wheelchair to push the door open it only budged a couple of inches. It must have weighed a thousand pounds! There was no way I could get enough power in momentum to shove it open.

"Luckily" a woman came down the hall at just that minute and offered her assistance. She got behind the wheelchair and shoved against the door while pulling me in but…strike number two against the building's designers: the door opened into a short entry to the bathroom which formed a sharp 90 degree angle with the doorway making it impossible for a person pulling a wheelchair in through the extra-heavy door to fit and make the turn! It was hard enough for just a wheelchair alone to do it! We had to do some fancy acrobatics to get us in the door and make the turn but we finally pulled it off.

Once I relieved myself I had to deal with a sink and soap dispenser that were meant for standing people and then faced, alone, that damned entry/door nightmare. I have to say I was tempted to just call it quits and make the bathroom my new abode. I had just started to pull the door ajar when I was saved again by another patron of the restroom. Then it was back onto that carpeted runway. By the time I reached the office door I was exhausted and frustrated. Another patient opened the door for me, (none of these doors had the handy pushbutton door opener for those of us who need the help. Did I mention that this was a *brand-new* building? And that I was going to see *an orthopedic surgeon*?) but the fun wasn't over yet. The receptionist counter where I was to check in was at "standing patient" height. Once again I would have to stare at the counter while talking to a voice on the other side.

I took my place in the waiting room. Shortly thereafter I was called back to the exam room but my wheelchair and I didn't fit! The small room was already filled up with an exam table, 2 chairs, the requisite cabinet with sink and a small table with a computer. There was no room for a patient in a wheelchair. The nurse had to shove the exam table up against the wall and remove a chair to get me in. (Did I mention that this was a *brand-new* building? And that I was going to see *an orthopedic surgeon*?)

Thankfully the news was positive. The new screws were where they were supposed to be and all was well. The PA then announced that I should continue with putting just the weight of the leg…wait, uh, *what*?? Are you sure? (I was remembering that many weeks prior when I first met with the surgeon that he had said that standard procedure was that by week 6 the patient could begin to increase the weight gradually. Now I was nearly 8 weeks out from the date of the fracture and *still* having to keep weight off??). The PA looked at my file and the surgeon's notes. Yes, that's what the surgeon had ordered.

I felt deflated. I know that in the grand scheme of things this was but a small blip. It's not like I was *never* going to get the use of my leg back. I knew that. But I had my 2-year-old grandson arriving in 10 days and I wanted to at least be "toddling" around like him by then. It's the little things…

A week later I had my second follow-up appointment, this time with the surgeon, and he declared that he had dictated his notes wrong before, that I could start putting more weight on the leg starting at 50% of my body weight.

Wait. Fifty-*percent*? David and I discussed this afterwards. Surely he was wrong again. Fifty-percent of my body weight was what my totally healed leg would bear. He must have meant fifty *pounds* of weight. Which is what I did until my next PT visit at which time I learned that what the doctor said was correct. Biology Lesson #38: when the human body takes a step with one foot the opposite leg is actually supporting, momentarily, the *whole* weight of the body. Duh!

I don't know which was worse. Steeling my patience for several more weeks of gradual weight-bearing or having to face the fact—and admit it to the world—what half of my body weight had become. I was already overweight when this whole circus started and once I broke my hip with no physical activity I had ballooned another 8 pounds to the highest weight I had ever been, even at 9 months pregnant!

But I was glad to be "back on my feet" again and would even test my limits a little by trying a bit more weight than I was allotted.

Jackie arrived to spend a month with us and I was reminded of my blog post so long ago when I announced that it was a race between my grandchildren and me to see who would walk first. How could I know then that I would be playing reruns a year later while they continued to make steady gains toward running, skipping and jumping?

Once Again in the Medical Care Gap

So, back in PT again I am also reminded of how easy it is to fall into the medical care gap. When I was graduated in December of the previous year and then dismissed again from PT in the spring I figured that was probably it. I was on my own and things were status quo. But it turns out I was wrong.

One of the first things my therapist asked me in our earliest visits was if I had been given stretching exercises[65] to do at home to counteract the hypertonicity. Well, I had been given strengthening exercises but not really stretching ones (and no one had mentioned that these exercises might help reduce the tone). She was aghast. So, one of the first orders of business was to start me on stretching exercises.

As I progressed she also brought up the dreaded AFO. Do I use it? *Infrequently.* Was I wearing it the day I fell? *No.* Why not? *It's uncomfortable and bulky and I feel like I have better control without it.* Then it sounds like you need a new AFO.

So, with her help—she knew more than I did about what I actually needed and could therefore talk intelligently to the technician who would design my personal brace—a few weeks later I had a new and improved personalized AFO. (Well, the verdict is still out on that one. My AFO designer was, I think, a bit optimistic when he said that if there was a special shoe I wanted to wear with it they could make it work. "Can you even dye my eyes to match my dress?!"[66] I mentioned my Ferragamos. He didn't know the name. The reality is that he's a dreamer. There's no way I'll be wearing those *ever* again—and especially with the Frankenstein AFO. That's what the "F" really stands for, you know.)

While I appreciated her help all along the way I was troubled by an overriding problem: I was caught in the medical gap *again.* In other words, if I hadn't fallen and broken my hip I

[65] Remember way back when I wrote about hypertonicity and that I learned that patients were supposed to have a team of folks helping them, especially with gentle stretching to prevent *contracture*?

[66] Come on, *Dorothy*...remember?? In the land of Oz? When they were getting dolled up to see the Wizard??

would not have landed back in PT. And if I hadn't ended back in PT I wouldn't have found out that my brace was now all wrong.

It is all too easy to fall into this gap more than once, particularly if the patient has multiple issues. In addition to the PT gap I think I mentioned that once my PT ended at Providence I no longer was the patient of my physiatrist who had been prescribing my Baclofen. To whom does that task fall now? To my primary care doctor who is a fine doctor but hypertonicity is not her *specialty*. She has to ask *me* how much I should be taking.

It's that word "specialty" that I think is responsible for the first kind of "gap"—the "hole." While the idea of doctors *specializing* in certain areas of medicine has doubtless often led to better treatment the concept has several holes in it—namely, holes between each specialty. In an ideal world, specialists would have a way to *coordinate* and *cooperate* with each other and services might even *overlap* somewhat. But, as we are all painfully aware, *this* is *not* an ideal world. In our medical world specialists tend to clump together in their cloisters of specialty and not "play well with others." If you're lucky, a specialist will share his/her notes with your primary care doctor, who by default becomes your overall health coordinator—but more often, just the repository for each of the records from all the specialists. No one is really *coordinating* all that care and the poor primary care doctor who tries to be the jack-or-jill-of-all-trades simply can't keep up with it all. Result? Patients frequently fall into the holes. Witness my experience with trying to move from in-home PT to outpatient PT.

Another result of specializing is that—I have to assume often out of necessity—specialists have tunnel vision. They know what they know and they know it very well. Beyond that, good luck. This was most painfully (in many ways!) self-evident when I had my first gall bladder attack. I thought it was my heart. The EMTs thought it was my heart. The emergency room staff thought it was my heart, so the hospital staff thought it was my heart. And that's all they checked. I went straight to the cardiac ward and they ran all the cardio tests (which, while an expensive way to do it, I have to say was an excellent way to get all those tests done in one fell swoop and get a clean bill of health for my heart.) but no one ever questioned that it might be something else other than GERD. If I had not been persistent I might not have been diagnosed and treated for my gall bladder beach.

Another kind of gap is the "ravine." This is where you see a specialist for a health-and-or-life-threatening event and you might see that specialist a time or two or three and then at some point they stop seeing you and let you fall into the ravine. My point is that some of us who have had these events still have the "appendage" that caused the event in the first place (e.g. Mattie with her brain tumors; me with my CCM). Just because they now lay dormant doesn't mean that they couldn't cause problems later, and what if they are secretly doing things that could lead to another event that might be otherwise prevented or dealt with before it becomes "an event." Also, you, as the impatient patient, might have *questions*! I mean, when you are first diagnosed with something unknown to you—and perhaps *unknowable*—you are just struck dumb. But as the weeks and months go by and you come out of your shock-fog you start to have questions, questions that simply aren't getting answered at WebMD. You might need the opportunity to check in with your specialist from time to time. And finally, while the rest of the world sleeps the medical world is making new discoveries. What if, say, someone uncovers a way to cure hypertonicity and I would miss out because I'm not rubbing shoulders with the specialist who might know about that cure because I'm stuck in the ravine?!

You've most likely heard of "GAP insurance"—Guaranteed Auto (or asset) Protection insurance [67] for cars. I think we need a kind of "gap insurance" for patients, a policy that would guarantee "Gap Avoidance Protection."

And Then, Depression Set In

One of my all-time favorite, endlessly quotable movies is "Stripes." "Stripes" has one of those scripts—not unlike much of Shakespeare's writing—that overflows with phrases that have crept into our vernacular as if we've been born using them. "Convicted? Never convicted." "No, but we're willing to learn. Will you send us somewhere special?" "I just wish I hadn't taken all that cough syrup." And my personal favorite: "And then, depression set in."

I've been on an anti-depressant since a year after my daughter was diagnosed with a brain tumor (now nearly 9 years ago). In that year we had ridden the medical roller-coaster of "let's-rule-out-a-tumor-I'm-sure-you-don't-have-a-tumor-oh-my-god-you-have-a-tumor-it's-cancer-it's-not-really-cancer-you'll-probably-need-surgery-we-can't-possibly-do-surgery-we-don't-know-what-to-do-you're-on-your-own. And we were still

---

[67] ...which "covers the difference between what the car is worth and what you owe on the car... if the car is stolen or totaled (damaged to the point that repair would cost more than the car is worth) while the owner is still making payments." About.com Cars

on it, going after every idea that comes down the pike.[68] On a routine visit with my general practitioner she asked me "how I was doing," meaning "emotionally," and I burst into tears. She took that as a big hint and put me on Zoloft.

Zoloft worked great for me. It helped smooth out the rough edges and even though I couldn't muster up tears very easily I was thoroughly happy. Until about 6 years later when I was in the throes[69] of menopause and began feeling suddenly suicidal. Once again, my GP was very astute and switched me to Pristiq. And I was on Pristiq during this whole stroke experience and wondered how much it might have masked how I really felt during it all.

Now I'm off Pristiq (recently as of this writing) so we'll see. But I can tell you either way, the reality—my new reality—is that sometimes the full impact of what I have left is downright depressing. And that's that. And that's all.

What We Have Here is a Failure to Communicate

During my last days of outpatient physical therapy, in a visit to my physiatrist he recommended that I begin tapering off of my Baclofen (the medication I had been on since PT began which was to help counteract the "tone"). As I recall, this information was being relayed through his physician's assistant, who informed me that the doctor determined that I no longer needed it. In response to my incredulous "why?" she said, "Because you don't have tone." Huh?!

---

[68] Pike is short for "turnpike" which is a toll road or expressway which got its name from the Middle English *turnpike* which according to Merriam and Webster was a "revolving frame bearing spikes and serving as a barrier." Huh?

[69] According to the Free Online Dictionary throes means "violent pangs of suffering." I'll bet you didn't know that either.

May Day

Let me get this straight. All along I had been told that I was battling tone after the stroke which made my muscles fight against the therapies they were trying to impose on them. Even as I improved and went through multiple iterations—and therapists—of physical therapies, I was informed that we were still working against "tone," which through my own research I discovered was short for hypertonicity. Yet this doctor of physical therapy had determined that I no longer had it.

I didn't get off of my Baclofen. I thought, even though he was a very kind man, that he might have been a tad batty. I was fairly confident in what the actual therapists were telling me. I have tone. And since he was no longer treating me because I was no longer receiving care from his physical therapy group I could continue my prescription through my GP.

But his diagnosis continued to dog my subconscious. What if he was right after all. Maybe I *don't* any longer have "tone," although after my hip fracture whatever this is seemed to get worse and increasing from 60mg back to my high of 80 mg seemed to help.

The reality is that even though I was technically on dose of 20 mg every 6 hours, once I was somewhat mobile again and busy with life I seldom remembered to take all of my doses. And then one day I forgot 3 of the 4 and decided to just stop altogether...just to see what would happen.

After a few days it occurred to me that I wasn't having trouble staying awake in front of my computer but I was also not going to bed instantly upon placing my head on the pillow. What now? Voilà! No Baclofen. One of the major side effects of Baclofen is that it caused me to feel a bit narcoleptic. As time went on thought, I felt that things were a bit worse and put myself back on Baclofen, first 20 mg, then up to 40 mg. I know I'm not really supposed to monitor my own medications but in the absence of clear communication from medical professionals that isn't contradictory I figure, what the heck?

Hope Against Hope

Okay, I'm the first to admit that miracles do *appear* to happen. People who have been given a death sentence by their doctors somehow manage to beat the odds. Healthy babies are born every minute in spite of the incredible hurdles they must overcome. The sun does come out on the very day that you planned an outdoor wedding.

But at what point do you get *real?* At what point do you just accept the hand you're dealt and stop looking for a better one? My post-fall PT does not seem ready to throw in the towel, mentioning possibilities like cranial sacral therapy or…? Her eyes light up almost mischievously when she talks about the "who knows?" options. It's easy to get caught up in her optimism.

And then I remember the point made by the immortal words of the character "Dr. Frankenstein" ("*That's* 'Fronkensteen!'") in the classic 1974 movie, "Young Frankenstein" by Mel Brooks: "…Dead is dead! ...Hearts and kidneys are tinker toys! I am talking about the central nervous system! … You have more chance of reanimating this scalpel than you have of mending a broken nervous system!"

We're talking about my *central* nervous system here. Yes, the brain can do some pretty amazing things—even accomplish "miracles"—when it comes to rewiring itself to compensate for damage done to its electrical circuit but, at a certain point, even the superhuman brain can't mend everything. Or can it...?

Oh, the Indignity of it All

If you did a search of the word "independent" in this book to this point you would find it used eleven times (10 in reference to me). But independent does not describe me completely and most likely never will. This fact is hard to swallow for a person who has come to cherish her independence over the years. Don't get me wrong. It's not that I refuse to ask for help; I'm willing to ask when I'm obviously in over my head but until that happens I prefer to swim on my own power. If I do a little self-psycho-analysis (which I am prone to do regularly) I think I can attribute this particular trait to being *learned* rather than genetic. While I am very much a "pack animal" I also have a keen sense of the "right" way to do things and have learned over the years that "if you want something done *right* you do it yourself." This is particularly true of the "pack" within which I have found myself. Besides, depending on someone else means possibly "putting them out" and those of us who are "feelers" are more concerned about others' feelings and keenly aware of others' opinions of us. Preserving those feeling and inspiring positive opinions take precedence over our own feelings and comfort.

I am also a fairly pragmatic person—or at least I seem to have become one. I think I can pinpoint the moment that that transformation happened. It was during the birth of my first child, a marathon of 36 hours that, in the end, involved all the beeping monitors, the salad spoons (forceps), threats of a C-section, and at least thirteen strangers staring at my crotch. It was at this point that I lost any concern or embarrassment over the indignity of so many people witnessing me at perhaps my worst.

The bottom line was that I wanted that baby *out of there* and all in one piece! At a certain point, for me anyway, all thoughts of propriety go right out the window.

Fast forward to my life now. I have had to swallow my pride—and any thoughts of independence with it—and asked for help from a friend and my sister-in-law (two women whom I believe to be uncomfortable with revealing body parts) to assist me with taking a shower. I have to rely on complete strangers to help wrangle my wheelchair and me into a bathroom. Getting in and out of a car can be a main event and sometimes require the assistance of someone to help bend and coax my right leg into submission.

For someone who is über-concerned about others' feelings the fact that I now inspire guilt on a regular basis is hard to swallow. People apologize for there *not* being any more handicapped-accessible parking spaces available. They apologize for forgetting to look for those spaces. They apologize for forgetting that the spaces with the access aisle on the right are the best for me and my uncooperative leg.

I am also keenly aware of the fact that my need to depend on other people means placing more of the burden on them. I have always been willing to accept more than my share of the load and pride myself on being fairly selfless. Not anymore. Others have to do all the driving now; others have to bring all the groceries in from the car; others have to do the heavy lifting. Where once I was the person who willingly took the innermost seat of a restaurant booth (sparing others the annoyance) I must now take the more prime positions.

For me, the only option for emotional survival of all of this—and more—is to take the pragmatic view. It is what it is. I have no choice (or few of them at best). Again, you have to laugh or…

This is not to say that I have given up my independent spirit entirely. I am also stubborn and—as I've declared before—the "Queen of Workarounds" so if there is a way that I can do something—no matter how difficult—I will figure out the way, even if I push the envelope at times.[70] And it is important that people let me have what little bit of independence—and the dignity that goes along with it—that I can manage. And that means being patient and sometimes waiting—something not well-practiced in this day and age. If you offer to hold the door for me, know that you are going to be there a *lot longer* than you might have anticipated. On the other hand, if it looks like I have a plan please don't offer to help me until it looks like my plan is failing. Often your offer to help comes across as a sign of your impatience with the situation. This is hard, I know. I am asking you to enter into the regular frustration that is my life. You didn't ask for this any more than I did but you are—like it or not—now an accomplice.

[70] Ever wonder what that phrase really means? Me too! It's an aeronautical phrase. Look it up: http://www.worldwidewords.org/qa/qa-pus1.htm

Epilogue

When does it End? (The book, I mean...)

I didn't intend to write this book yet, so soon after "it" happened.[71] I guess I thought I'd give it a couple of years to see how things would really turn out[72] so that I could legitimately write about all of it in the past tense. But friends would not quit nagging me about writing it. So I started writing not knowing at all how—or when—I would end it. (Hah, hah...I wrote these words before the hip fracture.)

I remember being truly flabbergasted while watching the "making of" documentary of one of my favorite films to learn that the director began shooting it without having a clue how the story was going to end. It amazed me that a studio could risk millions on a picture with so much uncertainty surrounding it. My son, who is a cinematographer, says this happens more often than we think. I guess if they can do it, so can I!

How will it end? Will the heroine get the guy? Will she be carried off on a big white steed to her new castle-home? I just don't know. I used to like this quote by Alan Kay, one of the fathers of the modern computer: "The best way to predict the future is to invent it." But given my current situation it seems so trite and even belittling. As if! I now have a new kind of future and I don't think I had much say in how it was invented. Nor do I have a clue what to expect next.

71 Although, given my post-stroke menopausal brain it's probably wise that I was "shoved" into doing this while some of it is still fresh!

72 Okay, you might call this procrastination. I call it wisdom!

May Day

There may be more options out there, new frontiers. I may try Botox. I might try to learn to drive with hand controls. Heck. I might live long enough that getting a bionic leg won't be out of the question. But for me there is a need to accept the current situation and figure out how to work with what I've got for a while. That is a fulltime job. It may sound like I'm "giving up" but at a certain point one has to put off dreaming and wishing and face facts. It actually can be the healthiest approach. Pragmatism is not a disease to be cured. I think finding a balance (even with one worthless leg) is the best solution.

However, you and I now are connected. You have read my book (unless you are one of those annoying folks who read the last pages of a book before you begin it in which case I relinquish any connection with you!) and now a piece of me resides inside your psyche. You can't help it and neither can I. It happens. My experience is now part of your memory banks and possibly even part of your emotions. If you are anything like me, once you learn so much about a person it's hard to just walk away as if nothing ever transpired between you. That's how I felt after reading Robert McCrum's aforementioned memoir or Suzy Becker's memoir, "I Had Brain Surgery; What's Your Excuse?" I truly appreciated their candor and willingness to draw me into the inner circle of their deeply personal experiences. But at the end of each book I felt at a loss. What happened to them *after*? That was then; what is now? What changes have taken place since they wrote those books? Inquiring minds really want to know! I mean, I feel like we're friends now and it's important to me to keep updated on their potential progress.[73]

---

[73] Of course that can backfire horribly as well. I read the chronicles of a young mother who suffered a stroke but the updates ended in 2005. I found out why by going to

Well, dear reader, I have great news! In anticipation of you feeling the same way now about me, I am inviting you to continue the journey with me. That's right! You and me. Come on along. It'll be fun!

You can follow my escapades at my blog: (iamawriterinmymind.blogspot.com) and you can even comment and ask me questions. How's that for "reader empathy"? But seriously…thanks for coming on the journey…

And remember…"every survival kit should include a sense of humor"[74]

her guest book where I got the unhappy news that she was killed in 2006 in an auto accident.

[74] Anonymous, whoever *that* is…

May Day

Further Reading

Becker, Suzy. *I Had Brain Surgery, What's Your Excuse*. New York. Workman Publishing, 2005.

McCrum, Robert. *My Year Off*. New York. Broadway Books, 1999.

Taylor, Jill Bolte. *My Stroke of Insight: A Brain Scientist's Personal Journey*. New York. Viking Adult, 2008.